Unlocking the Career and Technical Education Classroom

This guide provides a blueprint to bridge the gap between the business world and the educational world in your classroom. Whether you are a secondary teacher tasked with teaching business concepts or an industry professional teaching career and technical education (CTE) who is new to the school environment, these ready-to-implement strategies and resources make the transition an easy one. Following a "toolbox" theme, chapters outline the nuts, bolts, and other keys to success for those new to teaching CTE. Each chapter presents a different lesson for the business classroom, including personal stories, student quotes, material lists, steps to implement the lessons, assessment options, hints for success, and supplementary digital resources for you to download and use immediately. The author includes both classroom strategies and full lessons to make this your all-in-one solution to starting out in CTE. Ideal for both secondary business teachers and "second career" teachers entering the classroom from the industry side, this book helps reduce preparation time for new teachers and smooth the transition into this relevant and essential area of learning.

Ashley Johnson is a Career and Technical Education Teacher at Dekalb High School in Auburn, Indiana, USA, and a recipient of a Milken Educator Award with twelve years of experience teaching at the secondary level.

Also Available from Routledge Eye on Education
(www.routledge.com/eyeoneducation)

Teaching STEAM Through Hands-On Crafts: Real-World Maker Lessons for Grades 3-8
Christine Schnittka and Amanda Haynes

Introducing Engineering in K-8 Settings: Educator Tools to Support Children in Engineering Design
Elissa Milto, Merredith Portsmore, Christopher Wright, Chelsea Andrews

STEM by Design: Creating Strategies and Projects for Solving Real-World Problems in Grades 4-8, 2nd Edition
Anne Jolly

Turning it Around: Small Steps or Sweeping Changes to Create the School Your Students Deserve
Todd Whitaker and Courtney Monterecy

How to Get All Teachers to Become Like the Best Teachers
Todd Whitaker

Culturally Responsive and Sustaining Science Teaching: Teacher Research and Investigation from Today's Classrooms
Jamie Wallace and Elaine V. Howes

STEAM Teaching and Learning Through the Arts and Design
Debrah Sickler-Voigt

Empowering Students for the Future: Using the Right Decisions to Teach the Value of Passion, Success, and Failure
Eric Yuhasz

Teaching Students to Dig Deeper: Ten Essential Skills for College and Career Readiness
Ben Johnson

Unlocking the Career and Technical Education Classroom

Lessons for Real-World Learning in Grades 6-12

Ashley Johnson

Routledge
Taylor & Francis Group
NEW YORK AND LONDON

Designed cover image: Getty Images

First published 2025
by Routledge
605 Third Avenue, New York, NY 10158

and by Routledge
4 Park Square, Milton Park, Abingdon, Oxon, OX14 4RN

Routledge is an imprint of the Taylor & Francis Group, an informa business

© 2025 Ashley Johnson

The right of Ashley Johnson to be identified as author of this work has been asserted in accordance with sections 77 and 78 of the Copyright, Designs and Patents Act 1988.

All rights reserved. No part of this book may be reprinted or reproduced or utilised in any form or by any electronic, mechanical, or other means, now known or hereafter invented, including photocopying and recording, or in any information storage or retrieval system, without permission in writing from the publishers.

Trademark notice: Product or corporate names may be trademarks or registered trademarks, and are used only for identification and explanation without intent to infringe.

ISBN: 9781032900742 (hbk)
ISBN: 9781032900728 (pbk)
ISBN: 9781003546054 (ebk)

DOI: 10.4324/9781003546054

Typeset in Palatino
by codeMantra

Access the Support Material: www.routledge.com/9781032900728

Contents

Meet the Author vii
Online Support Material viii

1   **Introduction: My Journey to the Classroom** 1

2   **Entrepreneurship Unit** 5
    Quick Pitch Challenge • Microloan Program • Cost of
    Goods Sold/Break-Even Point • Business Fair

3   **Personal Finance Unit** 59
    Stock Madness • Children's Book Project • 30-Day
    Money Challenge • Simple Vs. Compound Interest

4   **Professionalism Skills Unit** 99
    Social Media Etiquette • How to Dress Professionally •
    How to Count Back Change • How to Write a
    Professional Email • How to Make a Professional
    Phone Call • How to Write a Check • How to Give a
    Professional Handshake • How to Write a Thank You
    Note • How to Address an Envelope • Professionalism
    Day • How to Tie a Tie • How to Iron or Steam a Shirt •
    How to Write a Check • How to Give a Professional
    Handshake • How to Make Change • How to Write
    a Professional Email • Social Media Etiquette •
    How to Make a Professional Phone Call • How to Write
    a Thank You Note • How to Address an Envelope

5   **Digital Career Portfolio Unit** 174
    Personal Narrative • Resume • Cover Letter • Letters
    of Recommendation • Community Service Project

6 Content Consumption Unit 216
Word Walls • Book Studies • Badges and Brags •
Article Annotations • Guest Speakers

7 Conclusion 258

Meet the Author

Ashley Johnson is Career and Technical Education Teacher with over 12 years of experience at the high school level. She started her career working in the radio industry holding titles like office manager, promotions director, and even on-air personality. After the closing of the radio station where Ashley worked, she was offered a job teaching high school business and hasn't turned back since. In 2013, Ashley earned her MBA from Indiana Tech in Fort Wayne, IN. She is married to her husband, Chad, and a mother to her daughter, Austyn, and son, Grant. Although she is best known for teaching Entrepreneurship, she has taught almost every business class available including Accounting, Management, Marketing, Personal Finance, Finance and Investing, Preparing for College and Careers, Digital Applications and Responsibilities, and Work Based Learning. Ashley has taken her students to multiple business pitch competitions over the years where her students have won over $20,000 in seed funding for their businesses along with many opportunities for college scholarships.

Online Support Material

Some of the resources in this book can be accessed online by visiting this book's product page on our website: www.routledge.com/9781032900728 (then follow the links indicating Support Material, which you can then download directly).

- Quick Pitch Challenge Materials
- Microloan Program Materials
- Cost of Goods Sold/Break-Even Point Materials
- Business Fair Materials
- Stock Madness Materials
- Children's Book Project Materials
- 30-Day Money Challenge Materials
- Simple vs. Compound Interest Materials
- Social Media Etiquette Materials
- How to Dress Professionally Materials
- How to Count Back Change Materials
- How to Write a Professional Email Materials
- How to Make a Professional Phone Call Materials
- How to Write a Check Materials
- How to Give a Professional Handshake Materials
- How to Write a Thank You Note Materials
- How to Address an Envelope Materials
- Professionalism Day Materials
- Personal Narrative Materials
- Resume Materials
- Cover Letter Materials
- Letters of Recommendation Materials
- Community Service Project Materials
- Digital Career Portfolio Materials and Rubric
- Word Wall Materials

- Book Studies Materials
- Badges and Brags Materials
- Article Annotation Materials
- Guest Speaker Materials

1

Introduction
My Journey to the Classroom

Growing up in Garrett, Indiana, several career choices crossed my mind, but not one of them was teaching. I was raised by an accountant and a banker, so business has always been in my blood, but I wasn't sold on it at first.

As a freshman in high school, I thought I wanted to do something in the medical field. Scrubs looked comfortable, and I knew I was meant to be in a position of authority. However, when my dad's appendix burst, I watched my sister pass out as the nurse wheeled my dad back into the recovery room after his appendectomy, I had a total meltdown.

In that traumatic moment, I realized (actually my sister and I both realized) medical careers weren't for us. Toward the end of high school, I landed on something in business. I really loved planning events and fundraisers. I even started a long running event for youth that teamed up with our local Relay for Life to raise money for cancer research during my senior year in high school.

I decided I wanted to work in marketing or promotions, preferably with a sports team. I have always loved baseball, especially the Cincinnati Reds. And that was the plan as I entered college. Or so I thought.

My sophomore year in college I won a radio contest and got to be the CEO of that radio station for the day and was paid an executive salary (for a day). After that day, they offered me an internship. I was able to see all areas of radio and how marketing and promotions really played a part in the industry. After the internship, I never left. I started working part time and eventually full time. I did everything from planning promotional events, working with the sales team, dealing with accounts payable and receivable, and even deejaying the midday shift (I had a cool radio name: Maggie).

After getting married and having my first baby, Austyn, I decided the crazy hours of radio were not really working for us. I started researching other careers that would work better for someone wanting to raise a family while having a career.

I have always loved learning, and on a whim one day started researching master's degree programs. I signed up that very day and began working on my MBA. While I had no idea how I was going to use this expensive endeavor, I felt good about the knowledge and personal growth. About halfway through the program, I learned with an MBA and one year experience I could get my teaching license; I would just have to get my Workplace Specialist license for the first year (I'm sure this isn't news to most of you. Many career and technical education (CTE) teachers are in their second career and were never formally trained to teach). Once I became aware of this information, everything seemed to click, and this became the new goal. I wanted to be a high school business teacher!

I was a little nervous to make the leap from radio to teaching. I could no longer hide behind Maggie's cool persona. I started looking for jobs to be a high school business teacher, but I wasn't in a hurry to make the change.

However, the universe had other plans. The radio station announced it was closing at the end of May. Ready or not: I was back on the job market. Someone was looking out for me, because at the end of July, just as my severance was running out, I got a job teaching high school business at a school about 40 minutes from my house. I was excited and extremely nervous.

The first few years of teaching were some of the most difficult I ever experienced, especially the first year. I don't think I slept well that entire year. While I had the industry experience on my side, learning the ins and outs of working in a school and the expectations of a teacher were hard. Learning targets, lesson plans, seating charts, discipline, repeat. It was all new to me and a huge adjustment. Most of the books and supplemental materials provided to me were outdated and not engaging. I wanted to create my own materials but found the time and effort to be a struggle. It would take me around three hours to put together an hour-long lesson. That first year I taught four different classes. Three hours for one lesson times four classes was 12 hours of preparation for a single day's worth of lessons. This didn't include grading or other reports I needed to do for administration. I received one hour a day for preparation during the school day. You don't have to be good at math to realize there were not enough hours in a day for me to accomplish what I wanted. The results were late nights, early mornings, long weekends, and many moments of feeling like I was failing. I loved what I was doing but felt inadequate.

After a few years of practice, I learned a lot and got better (and continue to get better) at all the things! I have experienced what students enjoy and can prepare lessons quicker. I have learned how to prioritize what is important and have gotten better at saying "it will be there tomorrow" (something every teacher can probably work on) and have developed rubrics and other ways to make grading easier and quicker.

I now teach seven different classes, lead other teachers, and sponsor two clubs. I continue to add to my arsenal of engaging and relevant lessons, but it takes me a fraction of the preparation time it did years ago.

Getting to a point of being comfortable and confident in my teaching ability was hard. And the reality is the struggle of the first few years is scaring great teachers away from the profession! We need great teachers who are industry experts teaching our kiddos. We need YOU!

I have been creating and updating my business CTE lessons and materials over the last 13 years, and I know many of you are in the same boat I was overwhelmed and short on time with a to-do list a mile long. You are industry experts but have been thrown into a classroom with little to no training and been wished "Good luck!" I want to help. I want to save you time, so you can focus on building relationships and providing engaging lessons with your students.

Over the next five units you will find different lessons to incorporate into your classroom. I begin each lesson with a short story of how the lesson came to be and then everything will be laid out for you: the materials you need, how I implemented the lesson, key hints to make the lesson successful, and the lesson materials. My hope is you will be able to implement these ready-to-use lessons in your class, engage with your students, and save some time! Use the lessons as is or make them your own. However you use them, I hope they will make your job a little bit easier and a lot more fun! (Figure 1.1).

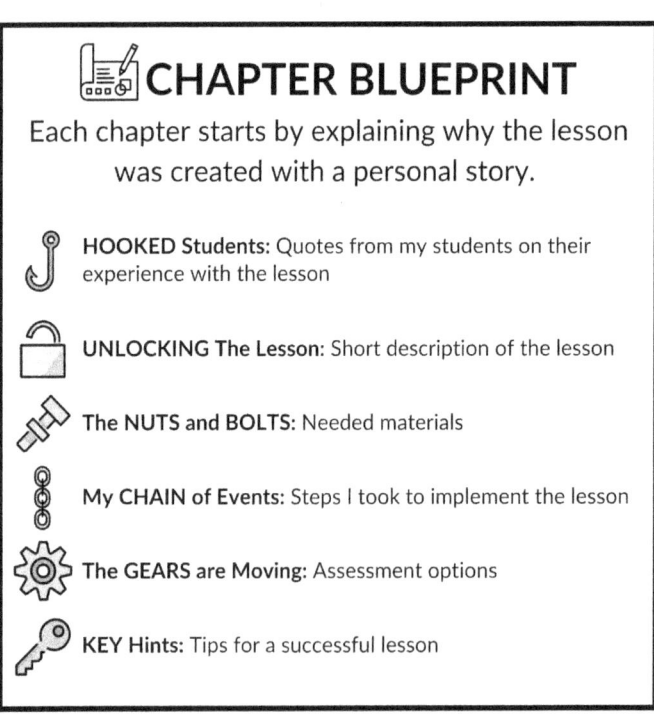

FIGURE 1.1 Chapter Blueprint.

2

Entrepreneurship Unit

Entrepreneurship is my absolute favorite class to teach. I see some incredible growth in students in this class, a lot of times from students who have always been told school is not for them. Whether a student goes on to start their own business or not, entrepreneurial skills are needed everywhere. Every industry needs go-getters who are innovative and willing to try new things. My entrepreneurship class and these lessons teach students to do just that!

The lessons in this unit can help break students out of their shell. By promoting the idea of "progress over perfection," students' ideas are validated, and they can really start to see the fruits of their labor. Some may even start making money with the projects they create. Right now, I have a student who made over $10,000 this past summer by power washing driveways. Give one or more of these lessons a try and see the confidence radiating out of your students!

Quick Pitch Challenge

Over the years, I have noticed the fear of not being perfect paralyzes students from getting creative, trying new things, and thinking outside of the box. Inspired by a board game, I created "The Quick Pitch Challenge" to help students put aside that fear.

When students are in elementary school, they are incredibly creative. Young students are willing to try new things, but as they get older, they start to care more and more about what their peers think about them. As they transition through middle school and into high school, they build up walls to protect themselves and creativity falls out the window.

Because of the time restrictions with this activity, students don't have time to think about failure. This process helps to knock down walls and allows them to get creative and have a little fun. We have had some crazy prototypes come from this activity: a fishbowl backpack to take your pet fish on a walk, a bike with pizza cutter wheels used to edge sidewalks, and earrings that hold your lip balm.

These silly "inventions" have bonded students and created a classroom atmosphere that allows for creative thinking without fear of being mocked.

 HOOKED Students

I feel like it was more fun working with people and trying new things.
~ McKayla R.

I liked the hands-on aspect of the activity.
~ Sam H.

 **UNLOCKING the Lesson: The Quick Pitch Challenge**

Get creativity flowing in the classroom. As a team building activity or as a starting point for a business idea, "The Quick Pitch Challenge" has students quickly go from idea to prototype in one class period.

 The NUTS and BOLTS

- ♦ "The Quick Pitch Challenge" material printables
- ♦ Timer

Entrepreneurship Unit ♦ 7

♦ An assortment of craft items to make prototypes (cardboard, construction paper, markers, tape, scissors, glue, clay, popsicle sticks, pipe cleaners, building blocks, etc.)

My CHAIN of Events

1. To prepare for the Quick Pitch Challenge Day, gather multiple craft supplies the students can use for prototyping.
2. Each student receives "The Quick Pitch Challenge" worksheet which includes the steps of the activity and the "Elevator Pitch" fill-in-the-blank.
3. Draw two cards. These are the two products students will need to combine to create a new product. Walk the students through the steps of the activity keeping to the time limits.

    a) **Individual Brainstorming**—*3 Minutes*—Students can sketch or write out details of their new product.
    b) **Feedback**—*2 Minutes each*—Students get two minutes to share their idea with a partner/group and record feedback (timing will be determined by how many students you have in groups. I try to keep it to 2 or 3).
    c) **Group Idea**—*3 Minutes*—The groups now have to come up with one product for the group. It can be an iteration of the group members' products or a combination of multiple group members.
    d) **Prototype**—*10 Minutes*—Each group now has to make a rough prototype of their product using the craft supplies you provided.
    e) **Pitch**—*3 Minutes*—Each group now has three minutes to come up with an elevator pitch for their product that they will present to the class. Students can use the "Elevator Pitch" fill-in-the-blank worksheet.
    f) **Present**—Have groups present their elevator pitch and prototype to the class.

 **The GEARS Are Moving**

The spirit of this activity is to get students to put aside their fear of failure. Because of this, if the students participate, they receive the points. I do not have a specific grading rubric for the activity.

 **KEY Hints**

- **Set the tone for the class.** I begin the activity by telling students, "You will create a prototype for an invention today. It may not be good, but by the end of this class, you can call yourself an inventor."
- **Have students vote on their favorite idea/prototype.** I usually supply a candy prize for the winning team.

Microloan Program

My most exciting class to teach is Entrepreneurship. While a lot of our lessons and projects are the same from year to year, what the students produce is vastly different each and every time. I am constantly amazed at some of the creative ideas these students pull out.

Local business pitch competitions are a staple each year. My students enter at least four business pitch competitions each year, many times walking away with cash to enhance their business. I LOVE business pitch competitions, and I LOVE when my students earn free money, but most importantly I LOVE the confidence and presentation skills students gain during these competitions.

In an effort to implement another lesson on business funding for my students, I teamed up with our local Chamber Foundation to start the Microloan Program. While free money from grants or business competitions is an amazing way to kickstart a business, it may not always be an option and there are other ways to fund a business. Businesses take out loans every day to kickstart operations. I wanted to present this option to my students as well to make our entrepreneurial journey reflect even more real-world relevancy.

Students go through the process of applying for a loan. A committee can approve or deny their application. If approved, the students are granted the loan to grow their business, but it is a loan. They must pay it back after an agreed-upon term.

Students quickly learn that they must prove they have a plan to make money in order to pay back their debt. The committee asks questions you would expect a bank to ask a business applying for a loan. It can be the scariest (according to the students) and eye-opening experience of our course. Students quickly realize if they have or have not prepared enough for their application interview.

 HOOKED Students

Getting a loan helps develop responsibility and real-world experience in dealing with a loan. This helps prepare us for our future.

~ Nash B.

 **UNLOCKING the Lesson: Microloan Program**

The Microloan Program provides young entrepreneurs with the opportunity to secure a small loan to kickstart their business ventures. Through this initiative, students can apply for funding to fuel their ideas while creating a relationship with a community partner and the local business community. By lending financial support and guidance, we can instill confidence in our students as they embark on their entrepreneurial journeys.

 The NUTS and BOLTS

- A community partner for funding
- Microloan guidelines
- Microloan application

My CHAIN of Events

1. First, find a community partner or source of funding for the project.
2. Establish a loan cap and set a due date for students to apply for the microloan.
3. With your community partner or an advisory board, go through the applications and decide which students will pitch for an opportunity at the microloan.
4. Set up a day with a panel of judges to listen to the pitches.
5. Have students present to the judges. Judges will then award a predetermined number of microloans to students they feel are worthy.
6. Have students sign the microloan agreement and award them the money.
7. Students then must pay back the loan after the agreed-upon time or fill out the optional "net loss" report if they were unable to make back the money.

 The GEARS Are Moving

Applying to the Microloan Program is optional in my classroom. Items required for the application are items students must complete for other aspects of my class; they just end up doing an extra interview with the committee. Students will be able to gauge their success by being granted the loan, building a business that is able to pay the loan back, and taking valuable lessons from the process (regardless of being granted or paying back the loan).

 **KEY Hints**

♦ **Find an option where you can have multiple community partners.** By creating a fund with your local community foundation or foundation at your school, you can have multiple community partners contribute to the fund for the program.

- ♦ **Put the decision in someone else's hands.** Have a committee of people from the community make the decisions of who gets the loans. This is helpful in three accounts: students tend to pay more attention and work harder when they know someone other than you will see their work; students are exposed to the local business owners, bridging a connection to the community; and you don't have to be the bad guy!
- ♦ **Have an alternate option for students who cannot pay back the loan.** No matter how hard you and the students work, it may be possible they don't make enough money to pay back the loan by the agreed-upon terms. Have an alternative requirement set up for these cases, we have a "net loss" report that has to be submitted in these cases. Students reflect on how they could have done things differently and what they learned from their experience.

Cost of Goods Sold/Break-Even Point

Every year I have students who have a great business idea and are ready to jump in with both feet. However, when it comes to pricing their product or service, 9 times out of 10 they price it way too low. Just telling them they have undervalued their business doesn't do the trick. You have to show them the numbers.

Students fail to consider the cost of materials, equipment, and even their time. One of the first things we do in Entrepreneurship class is to go over the Cost of Goods Sold and Break-Even Point. Once students have an understanding of how much it costs to make their product or how many items they need to sell just to make their money back, they quickly learn not to undervalue their business.

This quite possibly could be one of the most valuable lessons students can learn. They could be the most successful salesperson in the world, but if their product isn't priced right, their sales skills may not matter.

HOOKED Students

Learning how to calculate the cost of my product has really helped me plan how much I will charge people.
~ Saffron W.

 ## UNLOCKING The Lesson: Cost of Goods Sold/Break-Even Point

Before students can price a product, they need to understand Cost of Goods Sold and Break-Even Point. Give students these skills so they are better educated when pricing products and services.

 ## The NUTS and BOLTS

- Cost of Goods Sold/Break-Even Point lesson materials
- Building bricks
- Calculators
- Internet access for research

 ## My CHAIN of Events

1. I start with the "Cost of Goods Sold with Building Bricks" handout. Have students start by simply building a house with building bricks.
2. Then give students the handout. Have students disassemble their house to figure out how many of each type of building pieces were used.
3. Students will then calculate the "Cost of Goods" for building their house.
4. Next, have students use the "Cost of Goods Sold Making Pizza" worksheet. Students will do some research and find the cost of ingredients and calculate the cost of ingredients to make one pizza.
5. With students, complete the "Cost of Goods Sold and Break-Even Point" worksheet. Go over the definitions and calculations with the students as a class.

6. Have student individually complete the "Cost of Goods Sold and Break-Even Point" assessment.

 The GEARS Are Moving

Answer keys are included for the Cost of Goods Sold and Break-Even Point worksheets. I suggest reviewing the initial worksheet with examples with students and then letting them lose on the last sheet.

 **KEY Hints**

♦ **Have students build their house before you let them know what they are doing.** To prevent students from building a tiny house to get out of counting and figuring the cost, have them build their house out of building bricks before you introduce the lessons to them.
♦ **Add in labor calculations.** If you want students to get a feel of calculating labor, have them time themselves putting their houses made of building blocks back together. They can then use that time and assign a value per hour (or minute) to get an idea of adding labor cost.

Business Fair

Several years ago I started coaching students as they started their own businesses and competed in pitch competitions. The first couple of years a few interested students worked on their businesses outside of school hours and competed in one or two competitions. The last few years, I have been able to run multiple Entrepreneurship classes, and in addition to coaching dozens of students working through their ventures, students have competed in multiple pitch competitions as well as our school-wide Business Fair at the end of the year. Students have won their share in tens of thousands of dollars in seed funding. We have also teamed up with a local community college to offer dual credits. Multiple students have earned their initial Certificate of Entrepreneurship absolutely FREE!

Can you imagine having a class like this when you were in high school? Earning high school AND college credit while making money from a self-made business and earning free money from pitch competitions. Sounds too good to be true, but it's not. This class is the perfect motivation for some of my students. I have seen students with no interest in school whatsoever thrive in this environment.

 HOOKED Students

> Building my business has changed the way I want to live my life.
> ~ Connor W.

> I liked being able to make people happy with the items I made in my business.
> ~ Emma H.

> Building my business has allowed me to talk to adults within the community and get feedback about some of their ways for me to expand.
> ~Mariah W.

> I enjoyed speaking with community members and getting their opinion on my business idea.
> ~ Elizabeth J.

 **UNLOCKING the Lesson: Business Fair**

Inspire students to expand their entrepreneurial spirit by creating their own business. Take students through this hands-on entrepreneurial process from brainstorming to launching their own venture. Students will learn the ups and downs of starting a business which could produce real revenue.

The NUTS and BOLTS

- Science Fair boards
- Business Fair material printables

 My CHAIN of Events

The best part of this project is the fact that the time frame can be completely up to you. You can complete this project in two weeks or span it over an entire semester or school year. Running a business always has more work and refinement/updating. How detailed you want your students to get with this project is up to you. No matter how long you decide to do the project, the following lessons need to be implemented before the Business Fair can happen.

Problem/Solution

Have students carry the "Problems & Solutions" worksheet with them for a few days. They should write down problems they come across in their everyday life or things that bug them. Then they should come up with different solutions that could solve or make that problem better. They should go through this process for at least three days.

After students have a list of problems and solutions, they should use the "Solution Organizer" worksheet to sort and narrow down the problem and solution they will focus on for the project.

Business Name and Logo

Have students use the "Business Name and Logo" worksheet to do some research on colors and fonts. They will then come up with a business name and logo.

Mission Statement

Students should come up with a mission statement that will guide their business decisions. Use the "Mission Statement" worksheet to help students put together their statement.

Market Size

Use the "Market Size" worksheet to have students research the Total Available Market (TAM), Serviceable Available Market (SAM), and Serviceable Obtainable Market (SOM).

After coming up with a TAM, SAM, and SOM, students can put together a graphic with the template provided.

Students will use the "Customer Profile" worksheet to come up with their ideal customer and define their target market.

Prototype

Students will use the "Prototyping" worksheet to start coming up with their initial prototype. They will start with a sketch.

Students will then use whatever they can find (craft supplies, cardboard, etc.) to build their first rough prototype.

Customer Survey and Feedback

Have students use the "Customer Survey and Feedback" worksheet to come up with at least five questions to ask potential customers about their prototype.

Students should ask at least 50 people their survey questions and record their feedback.

The feedback data should be used to make iterations to their prototypes.

Marketing and Sales

Students will determine how they will communicate and distribute their product/service to their customers. Use the "Marketing and Sales" worksheet to determine communication and distribution plans. Then, students will put together some sample social media posts with the "Social Media" worksheet.

Business Model

Students will need to determine how they will make money and what their expenses will be. Use the "Business Model" worksheet to determine revenue and expenses.

Elevator Pitch

Students will need to prepare a 30–60 second elevator pitch that can be used for prospective investors. Students can use the "Elevator Pitch" fill-in-the-blank to help with this process.

 The GEARS Are Moving

The final assessment for students is the "science fair" style Business Fair where they get to give their elevator pitch and answer any questions one may have about their business. A rubric is attached for final assessment grading.

 **KEY Hints**

- **Start with the Quick Pitch Challenge!** Before challenging students with starting their own business, do the "Quick Pitch Challenge" to get the creative juices flowing.
- **Bring in community partners.** Have members of the community come to the Business Fair to act as judges. Ask if they would like to sponsor a cash prize and let them pick their winner to receive some seed funding. I always have five or six awards with money attached to hand out at the end of the fair.
- **Have other students vote on their favorite.** I invite other classes to come to the fair and vote on their favorite. At the end of the fair we present a "Student's Choice Award."
- **Utilize customer surveys/feedback throughout the process.** You can have students utilize surveys and feedback throughout the entire process: problem/solution, business name/logo, prototyping, marketing and sales.

THE QUICK PITCH CHALLENGE

Step ONE: Brainstorming

You have **THREE** minutes to **sketch** your product idea here:

Step TWO: Feedback

Each member of your group has **TWO** minutes to share their product and receive feedback. **Record** your feedback here:

Step THREE: Group Idea

After considering all products and feedback from the group, your team has **THREE** minutes to develop one product for the group. **Sketch** the group product here:

Step FOUR: Prototype

Your group will have **TEN** minutes to **build** a prototype of your group product from the supplies provided.

Step FIVE: Pitch

Your group has **THREE** minutes to develop an **elevator pitch** to convince the class to purchase your product. Use the Elevator Pitch Fill-In-The-Blank on the back of this sheet.

THE QUICK PITCH CHALLENGE

Copyright material from Ashley Johnson, *Unlocking the Career and Technical Education Classroom*, 2025, Routledge

Elevator Pitch Fill-In-The-Blank

Typically when _____
problem

people resort to _____
current way of solving problem

but _____.
why it's not good enough or could be better

Our solution, _____,
product/service name

helps _____
problem

by _____
description of how

_____
product/service is better

_____.

Quick Pitch Challenge Cards

Copyright material from Ashley Johnson, *Unlocking the Career and Technical Education Classroom*, 2025, Routledge

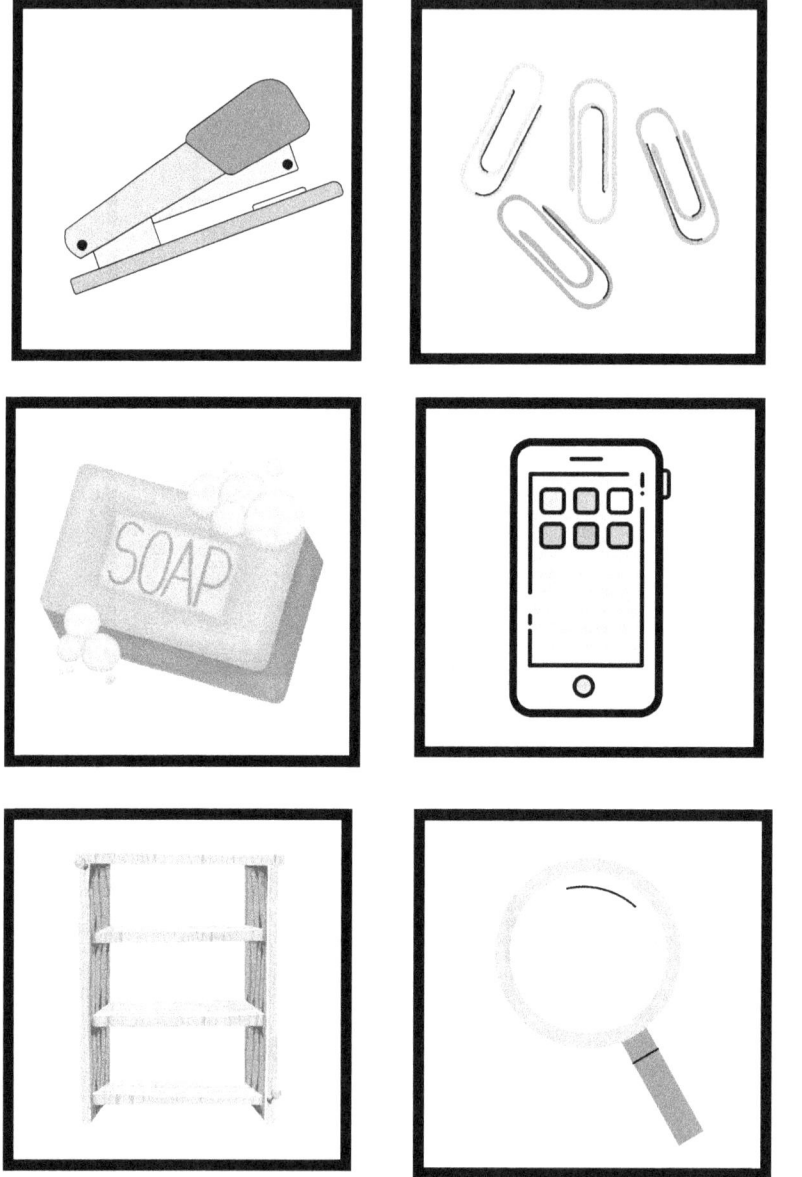

Quick Pitch Challenge Cards

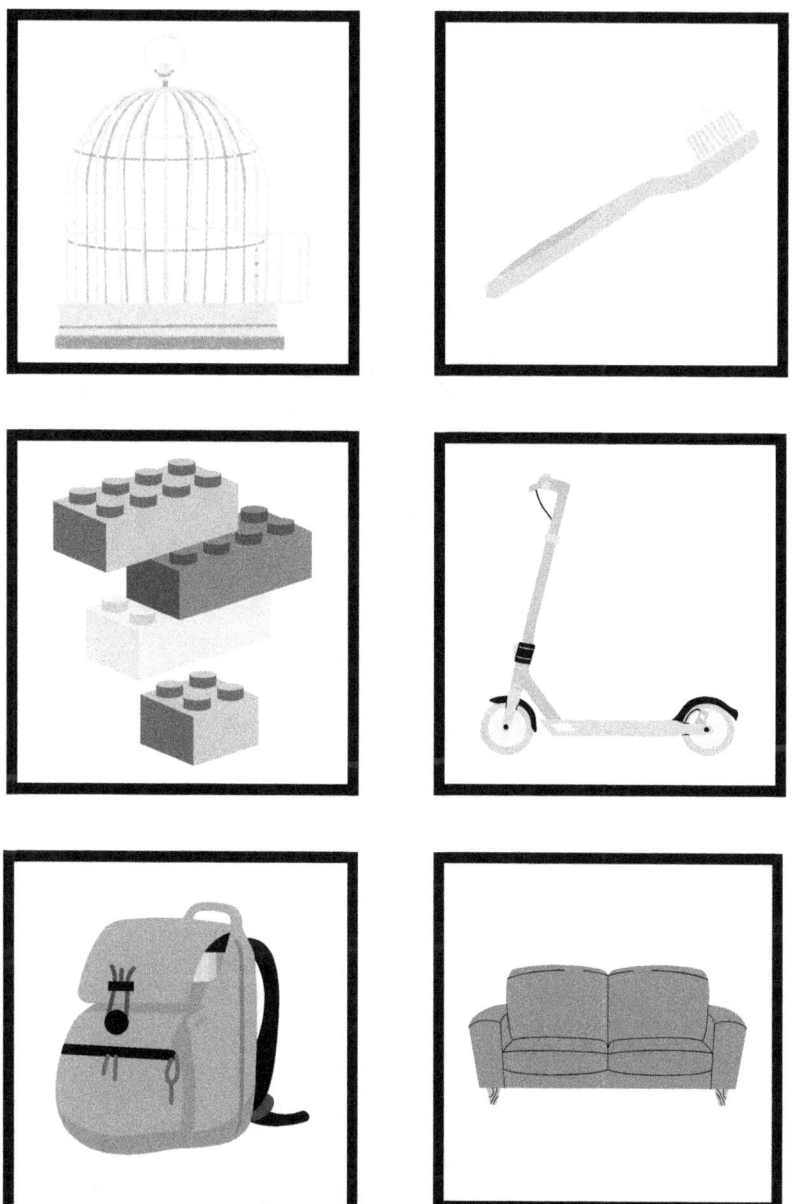

Quick Pitch Challenge Cards

Microloan Program

Microloan Program

Students are eligible to apply for a microloan in the amount of $100, $250, or $500 from the Microloan Program. Microloan funds are to be used toward the student's entrepreneurial business. Students agree to pay back the microloan within 90 days at 0% interest.

Microloan Program Process

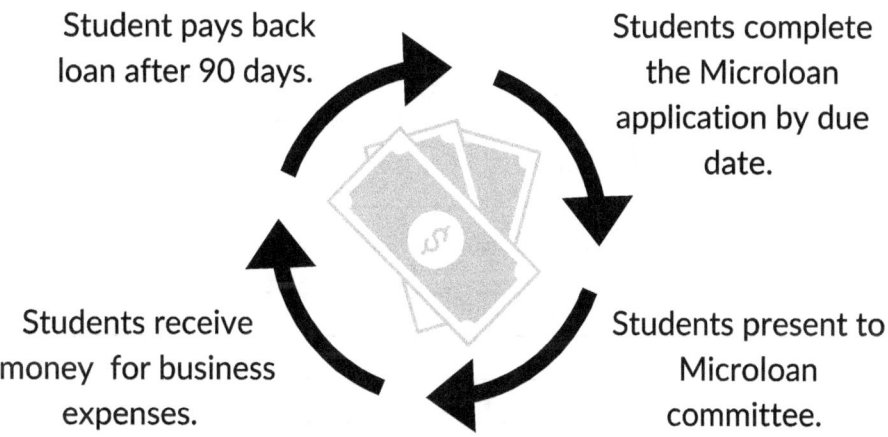

- Student pays back loan after 90 days.
- Students complete the Microloan application by due date.
- Students present to Microloan committee.
- Students receive money for business expenses.

Funding For Young Entrepreneurs

Application Deadline

_____

Microloan Program Application

Complete this application to be considered for a Microloan. Committee members will review the application and pick qualifying candidates to present (in person) to the committee. After students present, the committee will decide if they will grant the microloan request to the student/student team. Students can request $100, $250, or $500. Students agree to pay back the microloan within 90 days from the profits of their business or fill out a net loss report if their business was unable to produce profits to pay back the loan. If the student or student team is chosen to present to the committee they will need to complete a "Pitch Deck" and present to the committe at an agreed upon time.

Primary Contact _____

Additional Team Member Names _____

Primary Contact Email _____

Teacher Name _____

Teacher Email _____

Business Name _____

Loan Amount Request _____

Brief Description of your Business
_____
_____
_____
_____
_____
_____

What will you use the money for?
_____
_____
_____

Describe how you will be able to pay the loan back in 90 days?
_____
_____
_____

Microloan Program Pitch Deck

If selected to move on to the "Pitch Deck" round of the competition, students will need to put together a three to five minute "Pitch" that includes the following elements.

Pitch Deck
- **Title Slide**
  - Include business logo
- **Problem**
  - What problem is your business fixing or making better?
- **Solution**
  - How is your solution fixing or making the problem better? Why is it a better alternative to what is already out there?
- **Target Market/Market Size**
  - Who will be your customers? How many potential customers can you have?
- **Competition**
  - What else is out there to fix this problem? How are you different/better?
- **Business Model**
  - How do you make money?
- **Progress to Date**
  - What have you already accomplished?
- **Short Term/Long Term Goals**
  - What will you accomplish in the upcoming weeks/months/years?
- **Use of Funds/ How will you pay back the loan?**
  - What will you use the money for? How will you be able to pay back the loan in 90 days?

Pitch Date

Microloan Program Net Loss Report

If your business did not produce enough profits in the 90 days to pay back the full amount of the loan, please complete the following report.

Primary Contact _____

Additional Team Member Names _____

Primary Contact Email _____

Teacher Name _____

Teacher Email _____

Business Name _____

Loan Amount _____

Amount Repaid _____

What was purchased with the loan money?
_____
_____
_____

What was your original plan to pay back the loan?
_____
_____
_____

What went wrong in the plan?
_____
_____
_____

What did you learn from this process?
_____
_____
_____
_____

Copyright material from Ashley Johnson, *Unlocking the Career and Technical Education Classroom*, 2025, Routledge

Cost of Goods Sold & Break-Even Point

Copyright material from Ashley Johnson, *Unlocking the Career and Technical Education Classroom*, 2025, Routledge

Name _____ Period _____ Dates _____

COST OF GOODS SOLD WITH BUILDING BRICKS!

First, build a house out of building bricks. After you build your house, take it apart and calculate your Cost of Goods Sold using the pricing below.

Flat piece with (1-15 nubs) _____ pieces used X $1.50 (price per piece) = _____ Total Cost

Flat piece with (16 + nubs) _____ pieces used X $2.50 (price per piece) = _____ Total Cost

Regular piece with (1-6 nubs) _____ pieces used X $0.75 (price per piece) = _____ Total Cost

Regular piece with (7+ nubs) _____ pieces used X $1.25 (price per piece) = _____ Total Cost

Specialty Piece _____ pieces used X $1.75 (price per piece) = _____ Total Cost

_____
Grand Total Cost of House

Why is it important to know how much it cost for you to create your product?
_____
_____
_____
_____

Name _____ Period _____ Dates _____

COST OF GOODS SOLD MAKING PIZZA!

Find the cost of the items below from a local grocery store website. Determine how many pizzas can be made from the package and calculate the total cost of ingredients needed for one pizza. Then calculate the Total cost to make the entire pizza.

Refrigerated Classic Pizza Crust   _____ price   ÷   _____ # of pizza that can be made with a package   =   _____ Total Cost

Pizza Sauce use 14 Ounces   _____ price   ÷   _____ # of pizza that can be made with a package   =   _____ Total Cost

Mozzarella Cheese use 8 oz   _____ price   ÷   _____ # of pizza that can be made with a package   =   _____ Total Cost

Pepperoni use 2 oz   _____ price   ÷   _____ # of pizza that can be made with a package   =   _____ Total Cost

Canned Mushrooms use 2 oz   _____ price   ÷   _____ # of pizza that can be made with a package   =   _____ Total Cost

_____ **Grand Total Cost of Pizza**

Name _____ Period _____ Dates _____

COST OF GOODS SOLD & BREAK-EVEN POINT

The <u>cost of goods sold (COGS)</u> includes the price of each element of a product or service to get a total cost to create the final product or service.

The <u>break-even point</u> is when a business sells enough product or services to not lose any money. However, they also haven't made any profit. They have sold just enough to cover their costs!

Businesses have two types of expenses: fixed and variable.
Fixed Expenses are costs a business has to pay no matter how many goods or services a business sells. These are things like rent & equipment.

Variable Expenses are costs that change depending on how many products or services a business sells. These are things like materials need to build a product.

EXAMPLE:
You are starting a lemonade business at the local farmers' market for the summer. The cost for renting the space is $100. You also buy a sign, tablecloth, and a few other supplies to set up your stand. These items cost a total of $250.
Lemons cost $0.50 each, Sugar cost $3.56 for a 5lb (80 ounces) bag. Cups with lids cost $12.45 for a pack of 200. Straws cost $5.00 for a pack of 250. Ice cost $2.50 for a 160 ounce bag. You are able to get water for free at the farmers' market location.

IDENTIFY YOUR FIXED AND VARIABLE EXPENSES

FIXED COSTS	VARIABLE COSTS

CALCULATE THE COST OF ONE CUP OF LEMONADE

A batch of Lemonade makes TEN cups of lemonade. Here is the recipe for a batch of lemonade:
- 120 ounces of water
- 15 lemons
- 40 ounces of sugar

Each cup of lemonade will need to include the cup, straw, and 8 ounces of ice.

COST OF A BATCH

Water: 120 oz =   FREE
Lemons: 15 x $0.50 each = _____
Sugar: 1/2 x $3.56 (5lb bag)= _____
Batch Cost = _____

COST OF A CUP OF LEMONADE

Batch Cost _____ / ____ cups = _____
Cup/lid Cost _____ / _____ cups/lid = _____
Straw Cost _____ / _____ straws = _____
Ice Cost = _____ / _____ servings per bag _____
Cup of Lemonade Cost (COGS) _____

CALCULATING BREAK-EVEN POINT

*For the purpose of this exercise we will assume you are able to return any unused materials even if they are open.
*Round to the nearest cent and round up to the next whole cup.

1. **If you charged $2 for a cup of lemonade, what would be your break-even point?** _____

Calculate profits per cup

_____ − _____ = _____
Price charged   Cost   Profit
per cup   per cup   per cup

Calculate total fixed costs

_____ + _____ = _____
Summer   Both   Total
rent   supplies   fixed costs

Cups needed to sell to break even

_____ ÷ _____ = _____
Total   Profits   Cups needed
fixed costs   per cup   to sell to break even

2. **If you charged $2.50 for a cup of lemonade, what would be your break-even point?** _____

Calculate profits per cup

_____ − _____ = _____
Price charged   Cost   Profit
per cup   per cup   per cup

Cups needed to sell to break even

_____ ÷ _____ = _____
Total   Profits   Cups needed
fixed costs   per cup   to sell to break even

3. **If you charged $3 for a cup of lemonade, what would be your break-even point?** _____

Calculate profits per cup

_____ − _____ = _____
Price charged   Cost   Profit
per cup   per cup   per cup

Cups needed to sell to break even

_____ ÷ _____ = _____
Total   Profits   Cups needed
fixed costs   per cup   to sell to break even

Copyright material from Ashley Johnson, *Unlocking the Career and Technical Education Classroom*, 2025, Routledge

Name _____ Period _____ Dates _____

COST OF GOODS SOLD & BREAK-EVEN POINT ASSESSMENT

You are starting a lemonade business at the local farmers' market for the summer. The cost for renting the space is $175. You also buy a sign, tablecloth, and a few other supplies to set up your stand. These items cost a total of $235.

Lemons cost $0.35 each, Sugar cost $4.66 for a 5lb (80 ounces) bag. Cups with lids cost $11.25 for a pack of 200. Straws cost $7.70 for a pack of 250. Ice cost $2.78 for a 160 ounce bag. You are able to get water for free at the farmers' market location.

CALCULATE THE COST OF ONE CUP OF LEMONADE

A batch of Lemonade makes TEN cups of lemonade. Here is the recipe for a batch of lemonade:
- 120 ounces of water
- 15 lemons
- 40 ounces of sugar

Each cup of lemonade will need to include the cup, straw, and 8 ounces of ice.

COST OF A BATCH

Water: 120 oz =   FREE
Lemons: 15 x $0.35 each = _____
Sugar: 1/2 x $4.66 (5lb bag)= _____
Batch Cost =   _____

COST OF A CUP OF LEMONADE

Batch Cost _____ / ___ cups =   _____
Cup/lid Cost _____ / _____ cups/lid =   _____
Straw Cost _____ / _____ straws=   _____
Ice Cost = _____ / _____ servings per bag _____
Cup of Lemonade Cost (COGS)   _____

CALCULATING BREAK-EVEN POINT

*For the purpose of this exercise we will assume you are able to return any unused materials even if they are open.
*Round to the nearest cent and round up to the next whole cup.

If you charged $2.75 for a cup of lemonade, what would be your break-even point? _____

Calculate profits per cup

_____ − _____ = _____
Price charged per cup | Cost per cup | Profit per cup

Calculate total fixed costs

_____ + _____ = _____
Summer rent | Both supplies | Total fixed costs

Cups needed to sell to break even

_____ ÷ _____ = _____
Total fixed costs | Profits per cup | Cups needed to sell to break even

Name _____ Period _____ Dates _____

COST OF GOODS SOLD & BREAK-EVEN POINT

The <u>cost of goods sold (COGS)</u> includes the price of each element of a product or service to get a total cost to create the final product or service.

The <u>break-even point</u> is when a business sells enough product or services to not lose any money. However, they also haven't made any profit. They have sold just enough to cover their costs!

Businesses have two types of expenses: fixed and variable.
Fixed Expenses are costs a business has to pay no matter how many goods or services a business sells. These are things like rent & equipment.

Variable Expenses are costs that change depending on how many products or services a business sells. These are things like materials need to build a product.

EXAMPLE:
You are starting a lemonade business at the local farmers' market for the summer. The cost for renting the space is $100. You also buy a sign, tablecloth, and a few other supplies to set up your stand. These items cost a total of $250.
Lemons cost $0.50 each, Sugar cost $3.56 for a 5lb (80 ounces) bag. Cups with lids cost $12.45 for a pack of 200. Straws cost $5.00 for a pack of 250. Ice cost $2.50 for a 160 ounce bag. You are able to get water for free at the farmers' market location.

IDENTIFY YOUR FIXED AND VARIABLE EXPENSES

FIXED COSTS	VARIABLE COSTS
Rent	Lemons, Sugar, Cups/lids,
Supplies for Stand	Straws, Ice

CALCULATE THE COST OF ONE CUP OF LEMONADE

A batch of Lemonade makes TEN cups of lemonade. Here is the recipe for a batch of lemonade:
- 120 ounces of water
- 15 lemons
- 40 ounces of sugar

Each cup of lemonade will need to include the cup, straw, and 8 ounces of ice.

COST OF A BATCH

Water: 120 oz =	FREE
Lemons: 15 x $0.50 each =	$7.50
Sugar: 1/2 x $3.56 (5lb bag)=	$1.78
Batch Cost =	$9.28

COST OF A CUP OF LEMONADE

Batch Cost $9.28/ 10 cups =	$0.93
Cup/lid Cost $12.45/ 200 cups/lid =	$0.06
Straw Cost $5.00/ 250 straws=	$0.02
Ice Cost = $2.50/ 20 servings per bag	$0.13
Cup of Lemonade Cost (COGS)	**$1.14**

CALCULATING BREAK-EVEN POINT

For the purpose of this exercise we will assume you are able to return any unused materials even if they are open.
Round to the nearest cent and round up to the next whole cup.

1. If you charged $2 for a cup of lemonade, what would be your break-even point? 407

Calculate profits per cup

$2	−	$1.14	=	$0.86
Price charged per cup		Cost per cup		Profit per cup

Calculate total fixed costs

$100	+	$250	=	$350
Summer rent		Both supplies		Total fixed costs

Cups needed to sell to break even

$350	÷	$0.86	=	407
Total fixed costs		Profits per cup		Cups needed to sell to break even

2. If you charged $2.50 for a cup of lemonade, what would be your break-even point? 258

Calculate profits per cup

$2.50	−	$1.14	=	$1.36
Price charged per cup		Cost per cup		Profit per cup

Cups needed to sell to break even

$350	÷	$1.36	=	258
Total fixed costs		Profits per cup		Cups needed to sell to break even

3. If you charged $3 for a cup of lemonade, what would be your break-even point? 189

Calculate profits per cup

$3.00	−	$1.14	=	$1.86
Price charged per cup		Cost per cup		Profit per cup

Cups needed to sell to break even

$350	÷	$1.86	=	189
Total fixed costs		Profits per cup		Cups needed to sell to break even

Copyright material from Ashley Johnson, *Unlocking the Career and Technical Education Classroom*, 2025, Routledge

Name _____ Period _____ Dates _____

COST OF GOODS SOLD & BREAK-EVEN POINT ASSESSMENT

You are starting a lemonade business at the local farmers' market for the summer. The cost for renting the space is $175. You also buy a sign, tablecloth, and a few other supplies to set up your stand. These items cost a total of $235.

Lemons cost $0.35 each, Sugar cost $4.66 for a 5lb (80 ounces) bag. Cups with lids cost $11.25 for a pack of 200. Straws cost $7.70 for a pack of 250. Ice cost $2.78 for a 160 ounce bag. You are able to get water for free at the farmers' market location.

CALCULATE THE COST OF ONE CUP OF LEMONADE

A batch of Lemonade makes TEN cups of lemonade. Here is the recipe for a batch of lemonade:
- 120 ounces of water
- 15 lemons
- 40 ounces of sugar

Each cup of lemonade will need to include the cup, straw, and 8 ounces of ice.

COST OF A BATCH

Water: 120 oz =	FREE
Lemons: 15 x $0.35 each =	$5.25
Sugar: 1/2 x $4.66 (5lb bag)=	$2.33
Batch Cost =	$7.58

COST OF A CUP OF LEMONADE

Batch Cost $7.58/ 10 cups =	$0.76
Cup/lid Cost $11.25/ 200 cups/lid =	$0.06
Straw Cost $7.70/ 250 straws=	$0.03
Ice Cost = $2.78/ 20 servings per bag	$0.14
Cup of Lemonade Cost (COGS)	**$0.99**

CALCULATING BREAK-EVEN POINT

*For the purpose of this exercise we will assume you are able to return any unused materials even if they are open.
*Round to the nearest cent and round up to the next whole cup.

If you charged $2.75 for a cup of lemonade, what would be your break-even point? 233

Calculate profits per cup

$2.75 − $0.99 = $1.76
Price charged per cup − Cost per cup = Profit per cup

Calculate total fixed costs

$175 + $235 = $410
Summer rent + Both supplies = Total fixed costs

Cups needed to sell to break even

$410 ÷ $1.76 = 233
Total fixed costs ÷ Profits per cup = Cups needed to sell to break even

Copyright material from Ashley Johnson, *Unlocking the Career and Technical Education Classroom*, 2025, Routledge

Business Fair

Copyright material from Ashley Johnson, *Unlocking the Career and Technical Education Classroom*, 2025, Routledge

Business Fair Rubric

	Novice	Limited	Developing	Mastery
BUSINESS NAME AND LOGO	Business name and/or logo are missing.	Business name and logo are present. Little thought/effort when into design, fonts, or coloring.	Business name and logo are well thought out. Design, font and colors are enticing and easy to read.	Business name and logo are well thought out, clever, and catchy. Design, fonts, and color are easy to read and stand out in a good way.
PROBLEM/SOLUTION	No problem and/or solution is stated or is very unclear.	A problem and solution are stated but a bit unclear. No examples of consumers who struggle with the problem are given.	The problem and solution are clearly defined with examples of consumers who struggle with the problem.	The problem and solution are clearly defined with examples and research of consumers who struggle with the problem.
MISSION STATEMENT	No Mission Statement is present or is lacking in the business purpose, function, or goal.	The Mission Statement is present but the business purpose, function or goal is unclear.	The Mission Statement clearly defines the business purpose, function, and goal.	The Mission Statement clearly and passionately defines the business purpose, function, and goal.
MARKET SIZE	Market Size is not addressed in any way that can be understood.	A market size is addressed but not in the TAM, SAM, SOM format. Very little research has been done to come up with numbers.	The Total Addressable Market (TAM), Serviceable Addressable Market (SAM), and Serviceable Obtainable Market (SOM) are clearly defined in revenue per year. Research is clear.	The Total Addressable Market (TAM), Serviceable Addressable Market (SAM), and Serviceable Obtainable Market (SOM) are clearly defined in revenue per year. Research is clear. Information is displayed in a way that is quickly and easily understood.
CUSTOMER SURVEYS/FEEDBACK	No customer survey or feedback information was collected.	Very little customer survey or feedback information was taken into consideration during the iteration process. Little or no examples of surveys or feedback are given.	Customer survey and feedback information has clearly been taken into consideration during the iteration process. Examples of surveys and feedback are given.	Customer survey and feedback information have clearly been taken into consideration and used to pivot the prototype during the iteration process. Examples of surveys and feedback are provided and explained how they were used to iterate.

Copyright material from Ashley Johnson, *Unlocking the Career and Technical Education Classroom*, 2025, Routledge

	Novice	Limited	Developing	Mastery
BUSINESS MODEL	It is unclear how this venture will make money.	It is confusing how money will be made in the venture. Very little breakdown of revenue and expenses are provided.	A clear path of how money will be made is communicated. A detailed breakdown of pricing and expenses is clearly displayed.	A clear and detailed plan of how money will be made is communicated. A detailed breakdown of pricing and expenses is clearly displayed and easy to understand.
MARKETING AND SALES	It is unclear how customers will purchase the product or service.	A path to consumers is communicated but confusing as to how consumers will purchase the product or service.	A clear path to consumers is defined. It is understandable how customers will purchase the product or service.	Steps have been taken to define a clear path of communication to customers. It is clearly stated and understood how customers will purchase the product or service.
PROTOTYPE	No prototype or mockup has been created to clearly communicate the solution to the problem.	A very early idea prototype or mockup has been created. It shows the idea and purpose, but may be a bit unclear. The prototype somewhat solves the problem stated.	A prototype or mockup of the product has been created and clearly shows the idea and purpose behind the concept. The prototype solves the problem stated.	A working prototype almost ready or ready for sale has been created and clearly shows the purpose behind the concept. The prototype solves the problem stated.
ELEVATOR PITCH	Elevator Pitch is less than 15 seconds and/or is unclear on the problem being solved or why the solution is needed.	Elevator Pitch is between 15 and 30 seconds. Pitch is confusing and does not clearly state how the solution will solve the problem.	Elevator Pitch is between 30 and 60 seconds. Pitch is clear and concise, describes the problem and how the product or service is the solution needed. Pitch leaves the spectators wanting to know more.	Elevator Pitch is between 30 and 60 seconds (closer to 60 than 30). Pitch is clear and concise, describes the problem and how the product or service is the solution needed and is very conversational. Pitch leaves the spectators wanting to know more.
VISUAL APPEAL	Display board is unprofessional, messy, and hard to read.	Display board is adequate. Information may not flow as well as it should. Use of color, fonts, graphics, and pictures could have been better thought out.	Display board is professional, eye-catching, and easy to read. Use of color, fonts, graphics, and pictures makes sense and flows well.	Display board is professional, eye-catching, and easy to read. Use of colors, fonts, graphics, and pictures are done with extreme thought. Board could be used with potential investors.

Copyright material from Ashley Johnson, *Unlocking the Career and Technical Education Classroom*, 2025, Routledge

Name _____ Date _____ Period _____

Problems & Solutions

For one week, think of problems in the world or things that bother you and write them down. Come up with possible solutions that could help or fix these problems. After one week, you will sort your list to find one problem and solution to focus on for your business project.

Problem	Possible Soulutions

Copyright material from Ashley Johnson, Unlocking the Career and Technical Education Classroom, 2025, Routledge

Name _____ Date _____ Period _____

Solution Organizer

Take each solution that you and your team came up with and categorize it into one of the three boxes below.

Solutions I believe would work, and I have the means to implement.	Solutions I believe would work, but I don't have the means to implement.	Solutions I believe would NOT work.

Copyright material from Ashley Johnson, *Unlocking the Career and Technical Education Classroom*, 2025, Routledge

Name _____ Date _____ Period _____

Solution Organizer

Focus on the first two boxes. These are the solutions that you believe will work. Do not shy away from a solution just because you do not currently have the means to implement it. You can always find a way to implement it. Come up with the top 3 - 5 solutions you want to work with.

1.

2.

3.

4.

5.

Name _____ Date _____ Period _____

Business Name & Logo

Use this worksheet to brainstorm ideas for your business name and logo. Once you have an idea and sketch of what you want, make a digital version of your logo using your choice of computer software.

Business Name Options
You want something easy to read and catchy for your customers.

Logo Color Options
Colors can evoke different feelings from your customers. Do some research on the feelings you wish to target with your customers and the colors that go along with those feelings.

Logo Sketches
Does your logo make sense for the product/service you are selling? Make sure it is clean and can easily be transferred to marketing materials.

Copyright material from Ashley Johnson, *Unlocking the Career and Technical Education Classroom*, 2025, Routledge

Name _____ Date _____ Period _____

Mission Statement Worksheet

Use this worksheet to brainstorm essential pieces of information for your mission statement. Then, in two to five sentences, put the elements into a complete and concise statement.

Who/what is your business?	
What is the purpose of your business?	
Who are your customers?	
What needs are you fulfilling?	
Why is what you do important?	

Put it all together:

Copyright material from Ashley Johnson, *Unlocking the Career and Technical Education Classroom*, 2025, Routledge

Name _____ Date _____ Period _____

Market Size

Do some research to help determine the Total Available Market, Serviceable Available Market, and Serviceable Obtainable Market. Use the graphic on the back side of the page to create a visual of your Market Size. Record the sources from which you obtained your information.

Total Available Market (TAM)

What is the total market demand for your product or service?

Customers:

Sources:

Revenue:

Serviceable Available Market (SAM)

What is the segment of the TAM that represents your regional area?

Customers:

Sources:

Revenue:

Serviceable Obtainable Market (SOM)

What is the segment of the SAM that you can capture or handle?

Customers:

Sources:

Revenue:

Name _____ Date _____ Period ____

Market Size

Use the graphic below to create a visual of your Market Size.

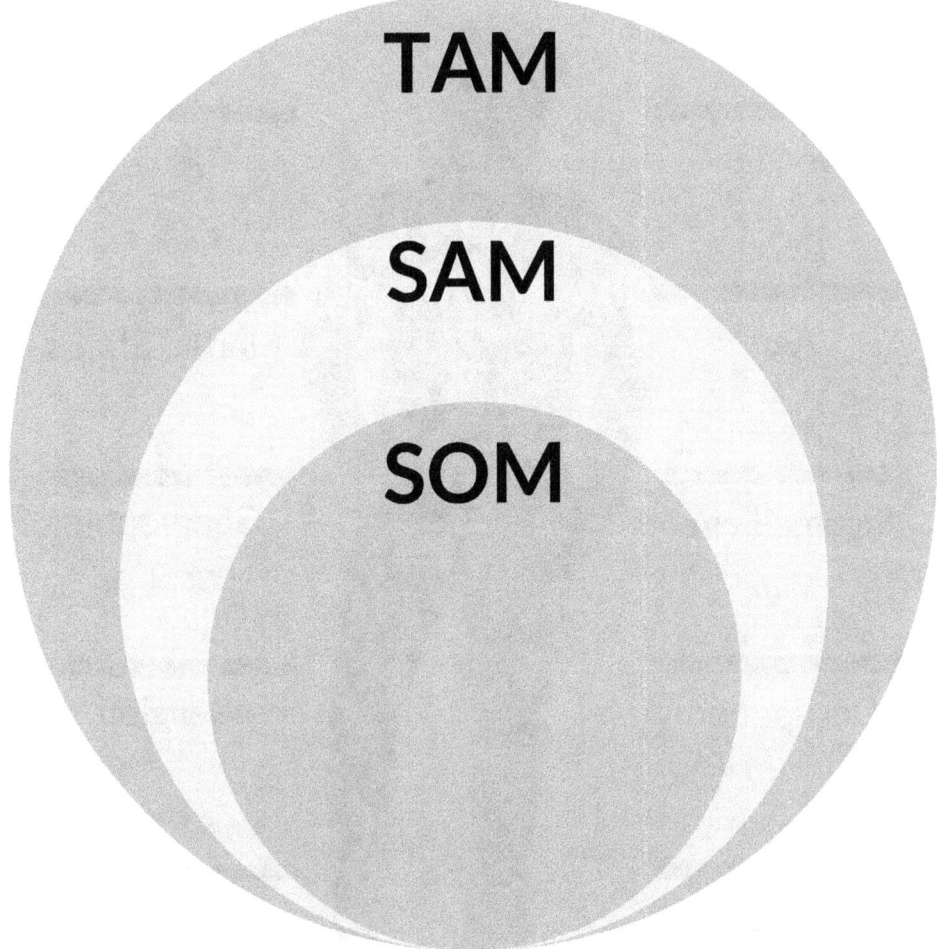

Name _____ Date _____ Period _____

Customer Profile

Record characteristics of your target customers. Remember the customer is the person who buys the product. They may or may not be the user of the product.

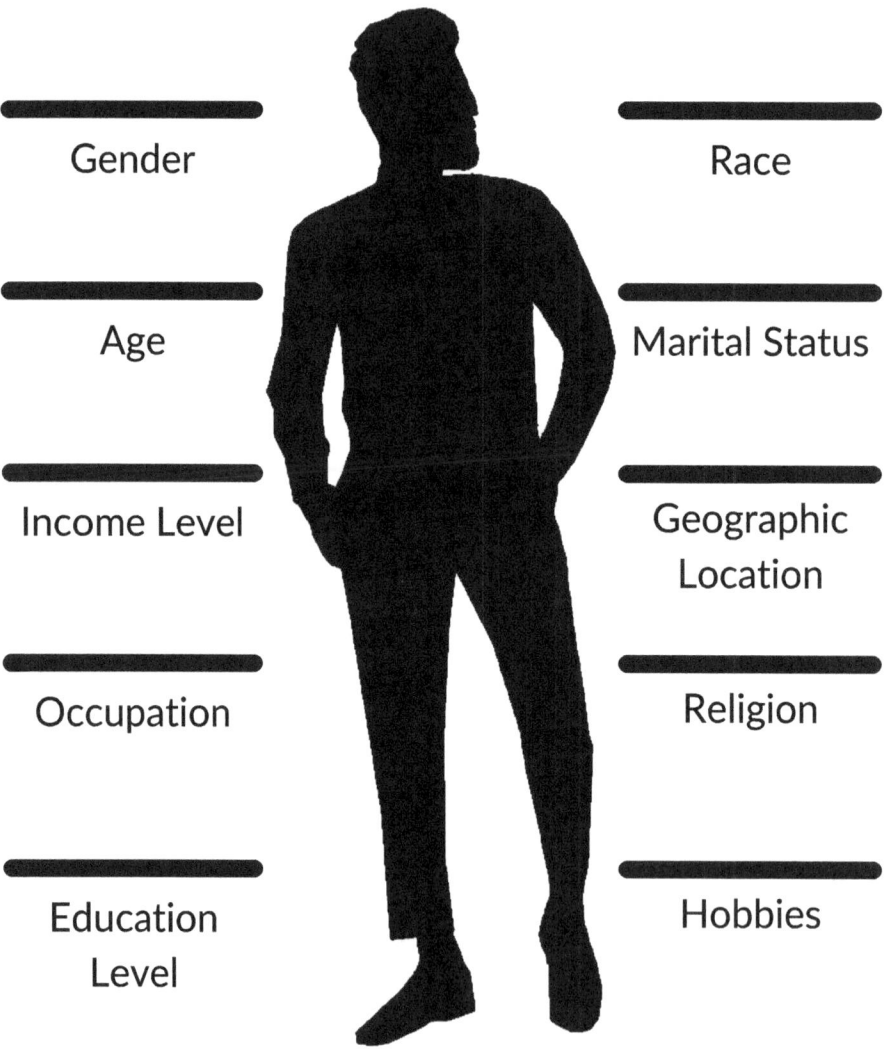

- Gender
- Age
- Income Level
- Occupation
- Education Level
- Race
- Marital Status
- Geographic Location
- Religion
- Hobbies

Copyright material from Ashley Johnson, Unlocking the Career and Technical Education Classroom, 2025, Routledge

Name _____ Date _____ Period _____

Prototype Sketching

Use the space below to start planning and sketching a prototype of your product or service. This can be a sketch of the product, app, website, or future building in which you will operate. Be sure to include special features that may be included.

Special Features:

Copyright material from Ashley Johnson, *Unlocking the Career and Technical Education Classroom*, 2025, Routledge

Name _____ Date _____ Period _____

Prototyping Round One

It is now time to create your first prototype. Keep in mind, this is the first attempt at your product or service. You will tweak and change this many times. Your first attempt will not be perfect, but you need something to start showing customers to obtain valuable feedback.

Your first prototype does **NOT** need to be functional. It just needs to give an idea of what you are thinking when it comes to your product or service.

If you are developing a product, here are some items you can use to develop your 1st prototype.

If you are developing an app, website, or service, here are some tools you can use to develop your 1st prototype.

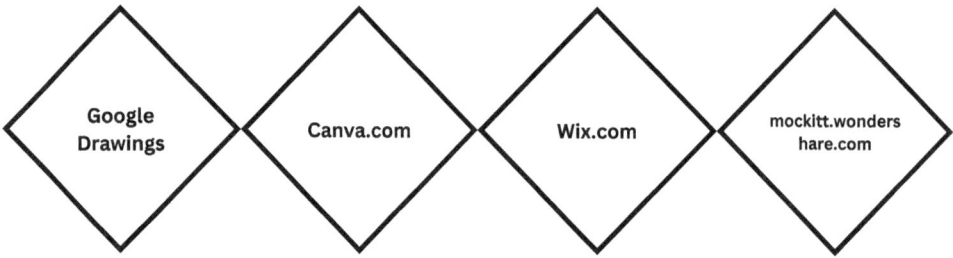

2

Copyright material from Ashley Johnson, *Unlocking the Career and Technical Education Classroom*, 2025, Routledge

Name _____ Date _____ Period _____

Customer Survey/Feedback

You will need to come up with at least five interview questions based on your prototype. You will need to survey at least 50 people. You will record their answers on the Feedback Form and use this information as you continue to make changes and develop your prototype.

Keep in mind:
- Is your prototype solving a customer's need?
- Is your prototype easy to use?
- What would your customer pay for something like this?

Question 1

Question 2

Question 3

Question 4

Question 5

Copyright material from Ashley Johnson, *Unlocking the Career and Technical Education Classroom*, 2025, Routledge

Name _____ Date _____ Period _____

Feedback Data

Record your Customer Survey/Feedback data here.

Question 1

Question 2

Question 3

Question 4

Question 5

Name _____ Date _____ Period _____

Marketing and Sales

You need to have a clear plan to get the products/services to your customers. It is best to have multiple channels of communication and distribution. Use the space below to plan how you will communicate and get the product/service to customers.

Distribution Examples:
Personal website, third party website, social media, personal store front, third party store front, direct to consumer, farmers' markets, craft shows, ect.

Channel 1	Channel 2	Channel 3

Copyright material from Ashley Johnson, *Unlocking the Career and Technical Education Classroom*, 2025, Routledge

Name _____ Date _____ Period _____

Social Media

Use the template below to draft a social media post for your business. Remember that the photo and wording of the post are equally important when drawing in your audience.

Social Media Site:

Topic of Post:

Key Words to use:

Name _____ Date _____ Period _____

Business Model

Use the spaces below to plan out your revenue streams and your fixed/variable expenses.

Revenue streams: How will your business make money? Note: Some businesses have multiple streams of revenue (For example: a tutoring service could make money on their tutoring sessions and on packs of flash cards they sell).

Fixed Expenses: What expenses do you have that stay the same no matter how much you sell?

Variable Expenses: What expenses do you have that will change as your sales change?

Name _____ Date _____ Period _____

Elevator Pitch Fill in the Blank

Typically when _____
problem

people resort to _____
current way of solving problem

but _____.
why its not good enough

My solution, _____,
product/service

helps _____
problem

by _____
description of how

_____
product/service is better

_____.

Copyright material from Ashley Johnson, Unlocking the Career and Technical Education Classroom, 2025, Routledge

3

Personal Finance Unit

Personal Finance is one of the most important classes a high school student will take. Everyone will have money to manage. Some may have a little and some may have a lot, but we all need to manage what we have. However, sometimes students feel like their time to manage money is so far away and they don't see the relevance of learning about it at 16.

The lessons in this unit can help bring Personal Finance to a level the students care about. Because they have an interest in what they are working on, they put in more effort and are more likely to remember what they have learned. Memorable lessons have the greatest impact!

Stock Madness

One of the hardest times to get high school students focused is around the time of the Division I Men's Basketball tournament. Spring break is in the near future and students who couldn't tell you the difference between a layup and a foul shot are suddenly interested in the tournament.

Years ago I started integrating the tournament into my Computer Apps Excel classes because there was no sense in fighting it. We were able to integrate a lesson on cell formatting and formula creation while watching the tournament in class.

I haven't taught Computer Apps in years but recently created an even more engaging lesson for my Personal Finance and Banking class called "Stock Madness." Again, if you can't beat 'em, join 'em. Students each invest a fake $100,000 into the competing teams as if they were businesses. They can invest everything in one team or divide their money up among a number of teams. The further their team, or "business," advances in the tournament, the greater their rate of return. We do this in real time as the tournament progresses and keep track of portfolio values after each round.

While integrating a current event that has the student's attention, you can introduce basic investing concepts that will stick with them for life.

 HOOKED Students

I was interested in the project because it involved something I was interested in.

~ Myles D.

It was fun learning about diversification in this way.

~ Ray C.

 **UNLOCKING the Lesson: Stock Madness**

Using everyone's favorite basketball tournament students gain an understanding of key investing terms and practices. By drawing parallels with investing and the tournament, students jump into topics of diversification, portfolio values, and risk while engaging in a fun classroom competition.

 **The NUTS and BOLTS**

- ♦ Stock Madness materials

My CHAIN of Events

1. Once the NCAA bracket is released. Fill in pages 1–3 with team names according to rank and the bracket.
2. Then, for every student, make copies of student "Stock Madness" packets (with your filled in teams) and the "Pre-Tournament" worksheet.
3. Instruct students to invest their $100,000 in as many teams as they wish. They must invest the entire $100,000.
4. Have students complete the "Pre-Tournament" worksheet explaining their investment strategy. Have students pair up and see how their investment strategies differ from others in the class.
5. After each round of tournament play, have students fill out their portfolio value in their student packets.
6. At the end of the tournament, students will calculate their final portfolio value and complete the "Post Tournament" worksheet. They will use this worksheet to create their final presentations for the project.

 **The GEARS Are Moving**

Students will use their answers from the "Post Tournament" worksheet to create a slideshow presentation on their investment strategies and results and reflect on what they would do differently if they were to do this project again. Students will also relate this project with investing in the real stock market (examples: Spreading investments among multiple teams represents diversification. Team seed rankings represent the investability of a company. The possibility of a star player getting sick or hurt represents risk).

 **KEY Hints**

♦ **Display the class rankings somewhere in your class after each round.** Students love a good competition.

By displaying the leaderboard in your class, you will keep the conversation going throughout the project.
- **Give small prizes after each round for the largest portfolio.** Have students figure their portfolio value after each round and give candy or small prizes to those who have the largest value.
- **Walk through portfolio calculations with students.** At least after the first round, make sure you walk through how to calculate their portfolio values. Sometimes students struggle to calculate the rate of return. I would walk through this process with them after each round to ensure they are calculating the right figures.
- **Display the bracket in your class.** I have a large poster of the bracket printed and displayed in the classroom throughout the project for us to fill in as the tournament progresses.

Children's Book Project

I have two children, Austyn and Grant, and throughout their childhood I have continuously looked for ways to incorporate money lessons in everything they do. My dad was always very open and honest about money and even took me to a seminar on mortgages when I was a senior in high school. Passing on a solid financial education to my children is on the top five list of my parental responsibilities. My kids will need to know how to handle money, whether they have a little or a lot, no matter what their career and no matter where they live.

As I was sorting through some old children's books dealing with money I had a lightbulb moment. What if I had my Personal Finance and Banking class write and publish a children's book on a Personal Finance topic?

Albert Einstein once said, "If you can't explain it to a six-year-old, then you don't understand it yourself." With this quote in mind, if my students could explain a Personal Finance topic to elementary school students, then they would develop a deeper understanding of the topic. Plus, by taking the books to our local elementary school and reading to kids, we could introduce younger students to important money lessons.

Producing a new book every year, each on a different money topic, builds a library of Personal Finance resources for our elementary classrooms. In our first year, my students took the topic of savings to write a story about a boy who got a piggy bank for his birthday and used it to save for a bike and later a car. We took a "book tour" and visited every second-grade classroom in our district. With the help of a community partner, we left a copy of the book we read in each classroom and each school's library. We also gave every student in the classes a piggy bank. The next year we visited all the second-grade classrooms again. The topic of the book that year was investing, and the students wrote a book about a little girl who invested her money in a slime making business. Again, we left copies of the books and, this time, gave every student a little jar of slime. This has turned into a fun tradition for my class and the second-grade students.

HOOKED Students

> I think I will remember this project. I haven't had any type of project like this in all four years of high school. Seeing how happy the students were and being able to interact with younger kids is always fun for me, so I really liked it.
>
> ~ Ashley R.

> Creating a children's book is like learning but in a more interactive way.
>
> ~ Allyson K.

UNLOCKING the Lesson: Children's Book Project

Empowering students to create a children's book on a specific Personal Finance topic drives them to understand the subject by teaching it to an elementary student. Taking the final book on "tour" makes the learning process genuine and authentic to real life!

 **The NUTS and BOLTS**

- Supplies for creating the books
- Children's Book Project materials

 My CHAIN of Events

1. Decide which topic/unit will drive this project.
2. After delivering normal instruction for that topic/unit, introduce the students to the Children's Book Project.
3. Depending on your class size, break students into groups (I have had classes small enough where the entire class worked on one book concept divided up by assignment, and I have had larger classes where students were put into four or five groups and each group worked on a book concept).
4. Using the Children's Book Project materials, have students go through the process of brainstorming, storyboarding, writing, and illustrating their books.
5. Handwrite final drafts and draw or develop on a computer program. You can bind them yourself; it doesn't have to be super fancy. However, if you want to go all out, see the Key Hints on how we took things to another level.
6. Set up a "book tour" with elementary classrooms.
7. FIELD TRIP! Take your students to elementary classrooms and have them read their final product to the kids. Prep your students with questions they can ask the kids about the subject of their book to increase engagement.
8. Follow up with the teachers of the classrooms you visited and ask for feedback (you can use the survey in the Children's Book Project materials).

 **The GEARS Are Moving**

Using the rubric provided in the Children's Book Project materials, an assessment grade can be taken. Also, use the feedback survey sent to the elementary teachers as a way to assess the success of the book tour event. Share this information with your students to give them a taste of new, real-life feedback instead of only feedback from you as their teacher. They get so much feedback from you that the third-party comments will really grab their attention.

 KEY Hints

- **Partner with a community member for funding.** Getting a community member to donate funding can allow you to purchase professionally printed copies of the books and a small gift for each elementary student. You can put the partner's logo in the book and include them in any social media posts or press releases.
- **Create "book tour" posters.** To build excitement, create "book tour" posters with the date on them to give to the elementary classrooms to hang.
- **Invite the press.** Celebrate your students and invite the newspaper and TV stations to cover your "book tour." Your students are amazing and the community wants to know what they are doing.
- **Reassure your students.** When hearing the news that they will be reading in front of classrooms full of children, my students tend to get very nervous. The elementary students think the high school kids are rock stars. Let your students know that by the end of the day, they will feel like Steven Tyler (or insert a name they might actually recognize).
- **Team up with an English teacher.** I team up with our Creative Writing teacher and have her class do peer

reviews on my students' book drafts. My students took feedback to make edits before preparing final drafts.
- **Take a class vote on one book.** When the class was larger and we had groups producing their own books, we took a class vote on the book that would get printed and taken on tour.
- **Leave gifts.** For each classroom we visited, we left a copy of the book and gave each student a small gift that was relevant to the story.

30-Day Money Challenge

Students (and most adults) are oblivious to their small daily spendings. I see students walk into my classroom EVERYDAY with snacks, coffee, and energy drinks. We all fall victim to the desires of small everyday pleasures and convenience.

It doesn't seem like much when you spend $4 here and $6 there. But it adds up. I'm guilty of it every time I go to Costco. I see cute organizational bins for $10, adorable little outfits for my nieces for $14, a year's supply of toilet paper for $50, and suddenly, I've spent $800. I'm sure some of you can relate.

Getting students to realize early in life, the domino effect of small purchases is important. It can be the difference between putting money away in a retirement, securing your future, and having to work into your late 70s. Starting early with savings is everything (see the compound interest lesson).

 HOOKED Students

I never realized how much money I spend getting snacks at the gas station.

~ Liz L.

I wasted money on things that caused me a lot of money that I didn't want to spend.

~ Peyton C.

Personal Finance Unit ♦ 67

 **UNLOCKING the Lesson: 30 Day Money Challenge**

Give students a glimpse of their spending habits with the 30-day money challenge. Students keep a record of their income and expenses for 30 days and classify each into categories giving them insight into how they spend their money.

 The NUTS and BOLTS

♦ 30 Day Money Challenge lesson materials

 My CHAIN of Events

1. Print and distribute "30-Day Money Challenge" logs to students. Explain to students that for the next 30 days they will keep a record of any income (allowance, salary, gifts, etc.) and any expenses (coffee, clothes, movies, etc.).
2. Once the 30 days are up, have students complete the "30-Day Money Challenge Reflection" worksheet to evaluate their spending habits.
3. Then, have students put together a presentation to give to the class. Students will include money goals, based on their evaluations, in their presentations and a plan on how to accomplish those goals.

 The GEARS Are Moving

Students will put together a presentation of their results from the "30-Day Money Challenge" to give to the class. A rubric is included to evaluate student presentations.

 **KEY Hints**

♦ **Print the log on colored cardstock.** To help prevent students from losing or ruining their logs, print them on thicker, colored cardstock. An electronic spreadsheet could also be made for students to keep their logs.

Simple Vs. Compound Interest

Compound interest is mathematical magic! It should be incredibly exciting to our students because they have the greatest factor on compound interest on their side, time! However, when talking about interest, the faces that stare back at you are usually anything but excited.

Trying to explain compound interest to students with words or numbers doesn't work. Their brains can't comprehend it. Heck, most adults can't comprehend it. To fully get your students to comprehend the anomaly of compound interest, you need a visual.

Having students watch interest, represented by beads, grow in two different jars (simple and compound) will give students a better understanding of how the two forms of interest work.

 HOOKED Students

It was surprising how much faster the beads in the compound jar grew!
~Julia M.

It was interesting to see how, after a couple days, the compound interest jar grew so fast.
~ Camilia R.

 **UNLOCKING the Lesson: Simple Vs. Compound Interest**

Give students a visual lesson on Simple vs. Compound Interest with beads representing the growing interest. Show the magic of compound interest as the beads in the compound interest jar grow faster than the beads in the simple interest jar.

The NUTS and BOLTS

- Simple Vs. Compound Interest lesson materials
- Two plastic jars
- Beads (at least 2000)

 ### My CHAIN of Events

1. Introduce students to the activity by showing the tracking sheets and labeling one jar "simple interest" and one jar "compound interest." Explain to students that to calculate simple interest you multiply the interest rate by the principle (the initial deposit) and to calculate compound interest you multiply the interest rate by the total number of beads in the jar.
2. On day 1, deposit 100 beads into each of the jars.
3. On days 2–30 calculate the interest for each jar and add the appropriate number of beads (round to the nearest single bead.) The calculated interest for the simple interest jar will be ten beads each day (10% multiplied by the initial 100 bead investment). The calculated interest for the compound interest jar will increase each day (10% multiplied by the total number of beads in the jar that day.) A cheat sheet that shows the number of beads needed for each day is included in the materials.
4. After 30 days, students discuss the difference in the number of beads in each jar and complete the Simple vs. Compound Interest reflection worksheet.

 ### The GEARS Are Moving

After 30 days of calculating interest and adding beads to the jars, have students complete the Simple vs. Compound Interest reflection worksheet. Based on their answers, evaluate if students took the lesson to heart.

KEY Hints

- **Make a poster out of the tracking sheet.** Put a large printout poster of the tracking sheet somewhere visible in the classrooms and fill it in each day with students.
- **Keep the activity going.** Keep the activity going for longer than 30 days and watch the compound interest jar explode.

"STOCK MADNESS" INVESTMENT BREAKDOWN

Name: _____

You have $100,000 to invest in "companies" during the "Stock Madness" competition. You can invest all $100,000 in one "company" or split your money between two or more of the 64 "companies" in the competition. Use the chart (below & on back of sheet) to distribute your $100,000 investment and create your portfolio. You must invest the entire $100,000. You will lose all the money invested for any "company" that loses in the first round of competition. For each "company" you invest in that makes it past the first round, you will earn the rate of return (indicated on the bracket) for the furthest in which the "company" advances.

WILL YOUR INVESTMENTS ALLEY-OOP OR AIRBALL?

Rank	Team Name	$$ INVST	Rank	Team Name	$$ INVST	Rank	Team Name	$$ INVST	Rank	Team Name	$$ INVST
1			1			1			1		
2			2			2			2		
3			3			3			3		
4			4			4			4		
5			5			5			5		
6			6			6			6		
7			7			7			7		
8			8			8			8		

"STOCK MADNESS" INVESTMENT BREAKDOWN

Rank	Team Name	$$ INVST	Rank	Team Name	$$ INVST	Rank	Team Name	$$ INVST	Rank	Team Name	$$ INVST
9			9			9			9		
10			10			10			10		
11			11			11			11		
12			12			12			12		
13			13			13			13		
14			14			14			14		
15			15			15			15		
16			16			16			16		

TOTAL OF ALL INVESTMENTS MUST EQUAL 100,000!!!

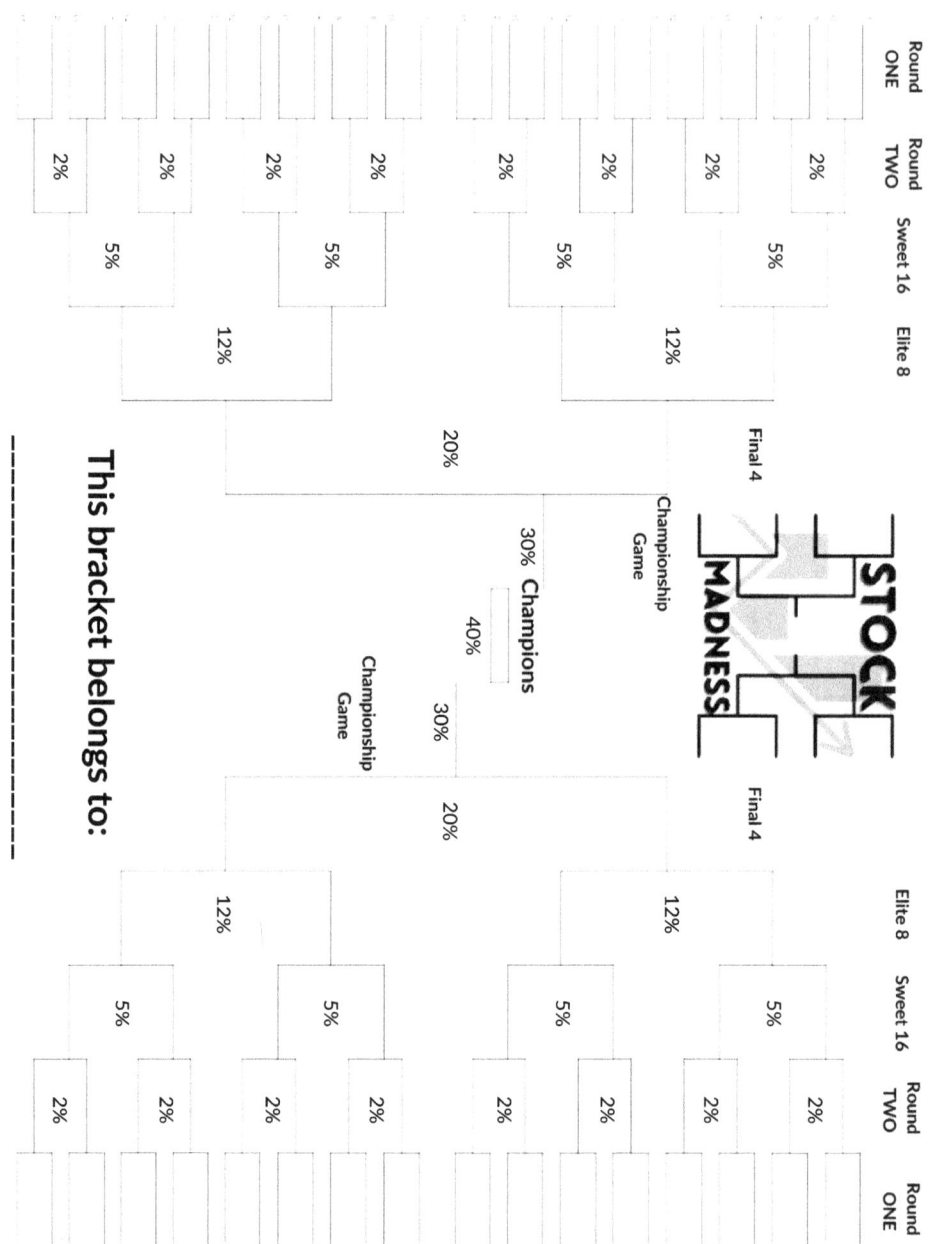

Name _____ Period _____

"STOCK MADNESS" INDIVIDUAL TRACKING SHEET

Use this sheet to keep track of your investment value. **REMEMBER**: You will lose all the money invested for any "company" that loses in the first round of competition. For each "company" you invest in that makes it past the first round, you will earn the rate of return (indicated on the bracket) for the furthest in which the "company" advances (example: A "company" that loses in the Sweet 16 Round will earn 5%).

After Round ONE:

List your stocks and their current values.
If your team lost in the first round, their value is ZERO. If your team won in the first round:
Original Investment x 1.02 = Current Value

Team Name	Current Value

Current Portfolio Value

After Round TWO:

List your stocks and their current values.
If your team lost in the second round, bring their value forward from the previous box and extend to all additional boxes. If your team won in the second round:
Original Investment x 1.05 = Current Value

Team Name	Current Value

Current Portfolio Value

After Sweet 16:

List your stocks and their current values.
If your team lost in the Sweet 16 round, bring their value forward from the previous box and extend to all additional boxes. If your team won in the Sweet 16 round:
Original Investment x 1.12 = Current Value

Team Name	Current Value

Current Portfolio Value

"STOCK MADNESS" INDIVIDUAL TRACKING SHEET

After Elite Eight:
List your stocks and their current values. If your team lost in the Elite 8 round, bring their value forward from the previous box and extend to all additional boxes. If your team won in the Elite 8 round: Original Investment x 1.2 = Current Value

Team Name	Current Value

Current Portfolio Value

After Final Four:
List your stocks and their current values. If your team lost in the Final 4 round, bring their value forward from the previous box and extend to last box. If your team won in the Final 4 round: Original Investment x 1.3 = Current Value

Team Name	Current Value

Current Portfolio Value

End of Tournament
List your stocks and their current values. If your team lost in the Championship, bring their value forward from the previous box. If your team won in the Championship: Original Investment x 1.4 = Current Value

Team Name	Current Value

Current Portfolio Value

HOW MUCH MONEY DO YOU HAVE AFTER THE TOURNAMENT?

Name _____ Date _____ Period _____

PRE-TOURNAMENT EVALUATION

After making investments in your chosen "companies", answer the questions below.

How many "companies" did you invest in?

Describe your investment strategy. Why did you invest in the "company/companies" you chose? What was your thought process behind the number of "companies" you chose?

Would you consider your investment strategy risky? Why or why not?

Would you say you have a: large, average, or small chance of making money from your investment decisions? Explain.

Does investing in a higher ranked "company" guarantee you will make money? Why or why not?

How does your investment strategy differ from others in the class?

Copyright material from Ashley Johnson, *Unlocking the Career and Technical Education Classroom*, 2025, Routledge

Name _____ Date _____ Period _____

POST-TOURNAMENT EVALUATION

After the tournament is over, evaluate your results and answer the following questions. Using information from this sheet, **create a slideshow presentation describing your investment strategy, results, and things you would change if you could do it again. Relate this activity with investing in the stock market.**

| Did you make or lose money? | After the results of this tournament, would you change your investment strategy if you did it again? Why or why not? |

| What was your rank on the class leaderboard? | |

| | What strategies were used by the students with the top three portfolio values in the class? What strategies were used by the students with the bottom three portfolio values in the class? |

| Describe the advantages and disadvantages of investing in multiple "companies"? | |

| | What factors of the tournament could have affected your results? How does this relate to investing in the stock market? |

| | How does this activity relate to making investments in the stock market? |

Copyright material from Ashley Johnson, *Unlocking the Career and Technical Education Classroom*, 2025, Routledge

"STOCK MADNESS" CLASS TRACKING SHEET

Keep track of students' investment rankings with the leaderboard below.

After Round ONE:
Student Portfolio Leaderboard

Name	Portfolio Value

After Round TWO:
Student Portfolio Leaderboard

Name	Portfolio Value

After Sweet 16:
Student Portfolio Leaderboard

Name	Portfolio Value

"STOCK MADNESS" CLASS TRACKING SHEET

Keep track of students' investment rankings with the leaderboard below:

After Elite Eight:
Student Portfolio Leaderboard

Name | Portfolio Value

After Final Four:
Student Portfolio Leaderboard

Name | Portfolio Value

End of Tournament:
Student Portfolio Leaderboard

Name | Portfolio Value

Name _____ Date _____ Period _____

"STOCK MADNESS" RUBRIC

	Novice	Limited	Developing	Mastery
LEARNING OBJECTIVE: Students are able to use the "Stock Madness" activity to connect key concepts of investing including: portfolios, risk, and diversification.	Student has **no understanding** of the learning objective. Student does not communicate any key investing topic (portfolio values, risk, or diversification) within the activity.	Student is **limited in understanding** of the learning objective. Student has limited communication on two or fewer investing topics (portfolio values, risk, and diversification) within the realm of the activity. Student does not connect topics to real-world investing.	Student is **approaching** the learning objective. Student communicates key investing topics (portfolio values, risk, and diversification) within the realm of the activity, but has little to no connection to real-world investing.	Student has **met** the learning objective. Student communicates **mastery** of key investing topics (portfolio values, risk, and diversification) AND connects elements of the activity to real-world investing.

Name _____ Date _____ Period _____

"STOCK MADNESS" RUBRIC

	Novice	Limited	Developing	Mastery
LEARNING OBJECTIVE: Students are able to use the "Stock Madness" activity to connect key concepts of investing including: portfolios, risk, and diversification.	Student has **no understanding** of the learning objective. Student does not communicate any key investing topic (portfolio values, risk, or diversification) within the activity.	Student is **limited in understanding** of the learning objective. Student has limited communication on two or fewer investing topics (portfolio values, risk, and diversification) within the realm of the activity. Student does not connect topics to real-world investing.	Student is **approaching** the learning objective. Student communicates key investing topics (portfolio values, risk, and diversification) within the realm of the activity, but has little to no connection to real-world investing.	Student has **met** the learning objective. Student communicates **mastery** of key investing topics (portfolio values, risk, and diversification) AND connects elements of the activity to real-world investing.

Copyright material from Ashley Johnson, *Unlocking the Career and Technical Education Classroom*, 2025, Routledge

Children's Book Project

Children's Book Project Brainstorming
Topic Brainstorm

You and your group will be tasked with creating a children's book explaining a topic we have discussed in class. Use this worksheet to brainstorm three different topics we have covered. For each topic, come up with three elements or subtopics that are associated with that topic. Then, narrow your options down to one topic to use to write your children's book.

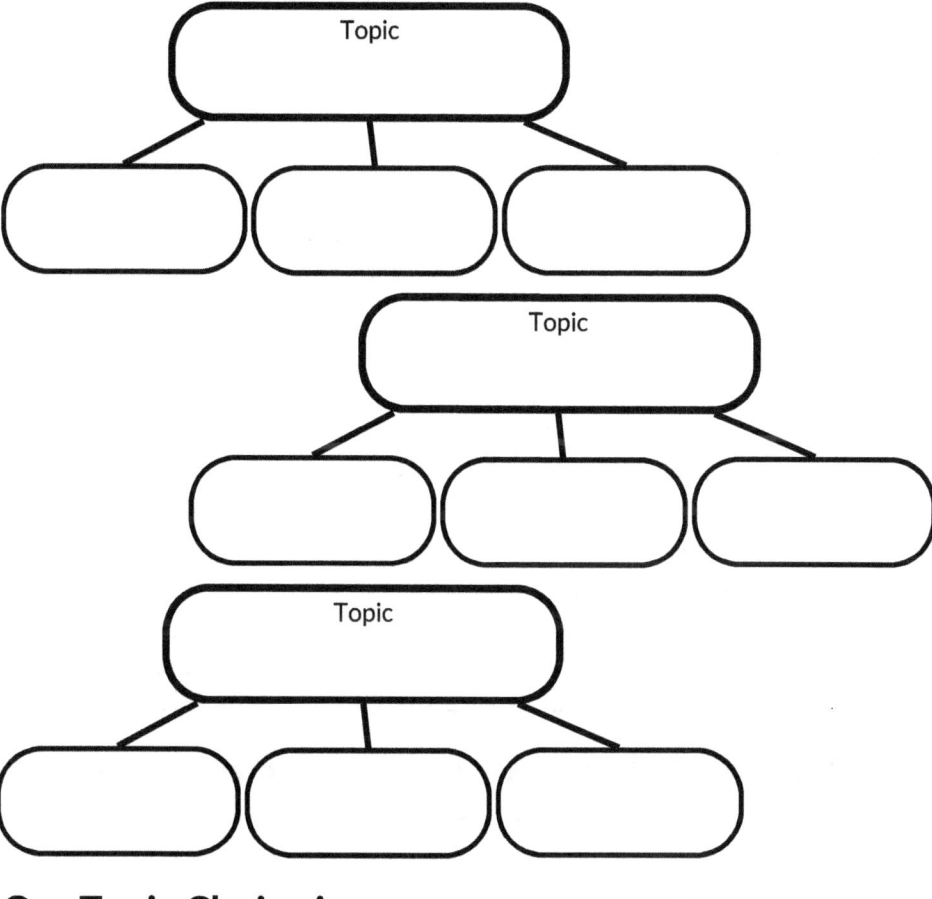

Our Topic Choice is _____

Children's Book Project Brainstorming

"If you can't explain it to a six-year-old, then you don't understand it yourself."
~ Albert Einstein

You and your group will be tasked with creating a children's book that explains a topic we have discussed in class. Remember, the story must be engaging and the topic must be explained in a way an elementary student can understand. You will write and illustrate this book. You will need at least 20 pages of text with illustrations. Use this brainstorming sheet and story board sheets to start planning your story.

The topic of this book is: _____
The grade level target is: _____

Who are your characters?
_____
_____
_____
_____

What will be the story line?
_____
_____
_____
_____
_____

What conflict will the characters overcome?
_____
_____
_____

How will you explain the topic in a way your grade level target will understand?
_____
_____
_____

Copyright material from Ashley Johnson, *Unlocking the Career and Technical Education Classroom*, 2025, Routledge

Story Board Template

Student Ballot

Based on the following criteria, select ONE Children's Book to represent our classroom on our "Book Tour" with elementary students.
- Easy to follow storyline
- Topic is covered with target grade level in mind
- Pictures complement and enhance the story

_____

Student Ballot

Based on the following criteria, select ONE Children's Book to represent our classroom on our "Book Tour" with elementary students.
- Easy to follow storyline
- Topic is covered with target grade level in mind
- Pictures complement and enhance the story

_____

Teacher Survey

Please rate the children's story presented to your students by ranking the statements below (1 - Strongly Disagree, 5 - Strongly Agree).

1. The story had a fun and engaging plot that my students could easily follow.
       1   2   3   4   5

2. The overall lesson (topic) was covered in a way my students could comprehend.
       1   2   3   4   5

3. My students really enjoyed having the high school students come visit and read the story.
       1   2   3   4   5

4. I would love for high school students to come visit my students again in future years.
       1   2   3   4   5

Children's Book Project Rubric

	Novice	Limited	Developing	Mastery
Plot: Is the plot easy to follow and engaging for the target grade level?	The plot is underdeveloped and does not engage the reader. Sequence of events is confusing. Not appropriate for targeted age group.	The plot lacks engagement and the progression of the story is disjointed. May not be best suited for targeted age group.	The plot is engaging and has a structure. There is a beginning, middle and end, but may have some pacing issues. Appropriate for the targeted grade level.	The plot is original, engaging and well developed with a clear beginning, middle and end. Appropriate for the targeted grade level.
Topic: Was the assigned topic covered in a way the target grade level could understand?	The story lacks a clear message of the topic. There is no lesson presented to the reader.	The story attempts to convey the topic but the lesson is somewhat unclear to the reader.	The story presents the topic assigned to the reader and integrates it into the plot and characters. A valuable lesson is presented to the reader.	The story clearly conveys the topic assigned. The message is integrated seamlessly into the plot and character development. A valuable lesson is presented to the reader.
Vocabulary/Language: Does the wording flow naturally and are the words used appropriate for the target grade level?	The writing is unclear and inappropriate for the targeted grade level. Language is not creative. Numerous grammar, spelling, or punctuation errors.	The writing is somewhat clear but lacks appropriate grade level vocabulary. Language is limited in creativity. Several grammar, spelling, or punctuation errors.	The writing is clear and appropriate to the targeted grade level. Language is adequate but lacks some creativity. Few grammar, spelling, or punctuation errors.	The writing is polished and appropriate for the targeted grade level. The language is creative and descriptive. Grammar, spelling, and punctuation are flawless.
Pictures/Layout: Do the pictures complement the text of the story and paint a better understanding of the topic?	The pictures are nonexistent or are poorly executed. They distract from the story or are inappropriate for the targeted grade level. Layout has no consistency.	The pictures do not fully compliment the story. They are acceptable but lack detail. Layout and design somewhat distracts from the overall appeal of the story.	The pictures are of good quality and compliment the story. They are appropriate for the targeted grade level. Layout and design are good but could be more refined or consistant.	The pictures are exceptional quality and compliment and enhance the story. They are appropriate for the target grade level. Layout and design are well executed.

30 Day Money Challenge

Name _____ Period ____ Date_____

30 Day Money Challenge Log

For the next 30 days, keep a record of all the money you earn and all the money you spend below. In the description, **categorize your income into one of the following categories: wages, allowance, gifts, or miscellaneous. Categorize your expenses into one of the following categories: food, entertainment, clothing, or miscellaneous.**

Date	Description	Money In	Money Out
-----	-------------	----------	----------
-----	-------------	----------	----------
-----	-------------	----------	----------
-----	-------------	----------	----------
-----	-------------	----------	----------
-----	-------------	----------	----------
-----	-------------	----------	----------
-----	-------------	----------	----------
-----	-------------	----------	----------
-----	-------------	----------	----------
-----	-------------	----------	----------
-----	-------------	----------	----------

Date	Description	Money In	Money Out
-----	--------------	----------	----------
-----	--------------	----------	----------
-----	--------------	----------	----------
-----	--------------	----------	----------
-----	--------------	----------	----------
-----	--------------	----------	----------
-----	--------------	----------	----------
-----	--------------	----------	----------
-----	--------------	----------	----------
-----	--------------	----------	----------
-----	--------------	----------	----------
-----	--------------	----------	----------
-----	--------------	----------	----------
-----	--------------	----------	----------
-----	--------------	----------	----------

Name _____ Period ____ Date_____

30 Day Money Challenge Reflection

Based on your "30 Day Money Challenge Log", answer the following questions.

Categorize Income

Calculate a total for each income category and create a pie chart representing the data.

Wages   _____
Allowance   _____
Gifts   _____
Miscellaneous _____

Income

Categorize Expenses

Calculate a total for each expense category and create a pie chart representing the data.

Food   _____
Entertainment _____
Clothing   _____
Miscellaneous _____

Expenses

What do you notice about your income/expenses?

_____
_____
_____

What changes would you like to make to your spending habits after looking at this data?

_____
_____
_____

Copyright material from Ashley Johnson, *Unlocking the Career and Technical Education Classroom*, 2025, Routledge

Name _____ Period _____ Date _____

30 Day Money Challenge Presentation

Using the information from your logs and reflection worksheet, create a presentation to give to the class.

Your presentation should include the following:
- Income category totals and details
- Expense category totals and details
- Personal spending trends
- Money Goals (at least three)

	Novice	Developing	Proficient	Advanced
Income	Student income is unclear or not communicated. No categories are given.	Student communicates income from their 30-day logs category details are non-existent or very messy.	Student communicates income from their 30-day logs with category details.	Student clearly communicates income from their 30-day logs with specific category details and a pie chart showing percentages for each category.
Expenses	Student expenses are unclear or not communicated. No categories are given.	Student communicates expenses from their 30-day logs category details are non-existent or very messy.	Student communicates expenses from their 30-day logs with category details.	Student clearly communicates expenses from their 30-day logs with specific category details and a pie chart showing percentages for each category.
Personal Spending Trends	Students personal spending trends are unclear and do not relate to personal habits and lifestyle.	Student identifies personal spending trends from the data they logged but does not relate it to their personal habits and lifestyle.	Student identifies personal spending trends from the data they logged and somewhat relates it to their personal habits and lifestyle.	Student clearly identifies personal spending trends from the data they logged and relates it to personal habits and lifestyle.
Money Goals	Student identifies 1 or no money goals for their future with no clear plan on how to implement them.	Student identifies at least 2 money goals for their future with a plan on how to implement them, but the plan may be a bit unclear.	Student identifies at least 3 money goals for their future with a plan on how to implement them.	Student identifies at least 3 money goals for their future with a clear and detailed plan on how to implement them.

Copyright material from Ashley Johnson, *Unlocking the Career and Technical Education Classroom*, 2025, Routledge

Simple Vs. Compound Interest

SIMPLE VS. COMPOUND INTEREST

For 30 days you will be comparing simple vs. compound interest. On day one you deposit 100 beads into each jar. Each day (Days 2-30) you will calculate your interest and add the corresponding number of beads to each jar *(round to the nearest whole bead)*. **The interest rate is 10%.** For the simple interest rate jar, each day, multiply the interest rate by the initial deposit (100). For the compound interest jar, each day, multiply the interest rate by the total number of beads in the jar.

	BEADS ADDED	SIMPLE INTEREST TOTAL BEADS	BEADS ADDED	COMPOUND INTEREST TOTAL BEADS
Day 1	100	100	100	100
Day 2	____	____	____	____
Day 3	____	____	____	____
Day 4	____	____	____	____
Day 5	____	____	____	____
Day 6	____	____	____	____
Day 7	____	____	____	____
Day 8	____	____	____	____
Day 9	____	____	____	____
Day 10	____	____	____	____
Day 11	____	____	____	____
Day 12	____	____	____	____
Day 13	____	____	____	____

Copyright material from Ashley Johnson, *Unlocking the Career and Technical Education Classroom*, 2025, Routledge

SIMPLE VS. COMPOUND INTEREST

	BEADS ADDED	SIMPLE INTEREST TOTAL BEADS	BEADS ADDED	COMPOUND INTEREST TOTAL BEADS
Day 14	____	____	____	____
Day 15	____	____	____	____
Day 16	____	____	____	____
Day 17	____	____	____	____
Day 18	____	____	____	____
Day 19	____	____	____	____
Day 20	____	____	____	____
Day 21	____	____	____	____
Day 22	____	____	____	____
Day 23	____	____	____	____
Day 24	____	____	____	____
Day 25	____	____	____	____
Day 26	____	____	____	____
Day 27	____	____	____	____
Day 28	____	____	____	____
Day 29	____	____	____	____
Day 30	____	____	____	____

Name _____ Period _____ Date_____

Simple Vs. Compound Interest

Based on the results from the Simple Vs. Compound Interest activity answer the following questions.

1. What is your biggest takeaway from this activity?

_____
_____
_____
_____

2. If you were earning interest on a savings account, would you want it to be calculated as simple interest or compound interest? Explain.

_____
_____
_____
_____

3. If you were paying interest on a loan, would you want it to be calculated as simple interest or compound interest? Explain.

_____
_____
_____
_____

4. When it comes to compound interest, explain how time is your best friend.

_____
_____
_____
_____

SIMPLE VS. COMPOUND INTEREST

For 30 days you will be comparing simple vs. compound interest. On day one you deposit 100 beads into each jar. Each day (Days 2-30) you will calculate your interest and add the corresponding number of beads to each jar (*round to the nearest whole bead*). **The interest rate is 10%.** For the simple interest rate jar, each day, multiply the interest rate by the initial deposit (100). For the compound interest jar, each day, multiply the interest rate by the total number of beads in the jar.

	BEADS ADDED	SIMPLE INTEREST TOTAL BEADS	BEADS ADDED	COMPOUND INTEREST TOTAL BEADS
Day 1	100	100	100	100
Day 2	10	110	10	110
Day 3	10	120	11	121
Day 4	10	130	12	133
Day 5	10	140	13	146
Day 6	10	150	15	161
Day 7	10	160	16	177
Day 8	10	170	18	195
Day 9	10	180	20	215
Day 10	10	190	22	237
Day 11	10	200	24	261
Day 12	10	210	26	287
Day 13	10	220	29	316

SIMPLE VS. COMPOUND INTEREST

	BEADS ADDED	SIMPLE INTEREST TOTAL BEADS	BEADS ADDED	COMPOUND INTEREST TOTAL BEADS
Day 14	10	230	32	348
Day 15	10	240	35	383
Day 16	10	250	38	421
Day 17	10	260	42	463
Day 18	10	270	46	509
Day 19	10	280	51	560
Day 20	10	290	56	616
Day 21	10	300	62	678
Day 22	10	310	68	746
Day 23	10	320	75	821
Day 24	10	330	82	903
Day 25	10	340	90	993
Day 26	10	350	99	1092
Day 27	10	360	109	1201
Day 28	10	370	120	1321
Day 29	10	380	132	1453
Day 30	10	390	145	1598

Copyright material from Ashley Johnson, *Unlocking the Career and Technical Education Classroom*, 2025, Routledge

4

Professionalism Skills Unit

In a high school classroom, I never would have guessed I would have to teach students how to complete certain skills over the year (making a phone call, mailing a letter, writing a thank you note). But after thinking, I realized these students probably had very little reason to send a letter along with some of these other skills. Technology has advanced, and what once was a common skill has become a sporadic need. Certain skills are not used as often as they once were, but it does not mean they are not important or needed.

This unit includes nine different professionalism lessons to use as you choose with your students. They are designed to be standalone lessons or use them to lead up to a Professionalism Day event. Or, if you are short on time, skip right to the Professionals Day stations to give your students a taste of each skill. Professionalism Day Stations and student worksheets are included in the materials.

Social Media Etiquette

It's not news to anyone that our students (many adults too) need a lesson on social media etiquette. Technology progressed so quickly, never truly giving us time to develop professional norms. Society has just gotten used to posting everything and anything online. Our students are the first generation to not know a life without social media. They have grown up watching the lives of their favorite celebrities, friends, and classmates from the palm of their hand.

Whie it is still a fairly new concept for colleges and employers to review the social media accounts of their applicants; it is happening, and it is growing, fast! More and more we see on the news students who have lost scholarships and employees who have lost jobs because of social media posts.

We need to educate our students on proper social media guidelines, not only to apply to colleges and start their careers but also to keep them safe. The number of cyber scams and child solicitations and abductions continues to grow year after year.

HOOKED Students

> I don't always think about what other people may think about my posts, but probably should.
>
> ~ Addie T.

> I feel like these are things everyone should know, but they don't.
>
> ~ Marissa M.

UNLOCKING the Lesson: Social Media Etiquette

Moving forward in life, students will be judged on their social media for many reasons including college acceptance and employment opportunities. Review some simple tips for social media to help students stand out in a positive way with their social media.

The NUTS and BOLTS

- Social Media Etiquette lesson materials

My CHAIN of Events

1. Review the "Social Media Etiquette" handout with students.
2. Have students complete the "Social Media Etiquette" card sort. Students will sort the social media posts into two categories: appropriate and not appropriate.
3. Have students complete the card sort reflection worksheet and describe why they placed each social media post into each category.

 The GEARS Are Moving

Review the card sort reflection worksheet for each student to see where they sorted the social media posts and why they put each post into each category.

 **KEY Hints**

♦ **Find online examples of unprofessional social media posts.** Find some unprofessional posts from celebrities or politicians and review them with your students.

How to Dress Professionally

I don't know if I'm getting older or if kids care less and less about what they wear. Sweatpants and t-shirts seem to be the new teenage uniform. Wearing jeans seems to be dressing up for most students these days.

Over the last couple of years, I have found that I need to be very specific when I need students to dress professionally. I used to be able to say, "dress professionally," and all word be ok. Now I need to be more specific. Sometimes I'll take students to events and some of the phrases I need to use to get students to dress professionally include, "no sweatpants," "no shorts," "no band t-shirts," and "no socks with sandals." The last one kills me.

When I was in school, if you wore socks with sandals you were a middle-aged soccer dad driving a mini-van. Now, it's all the kids wear!

A little review of what is appropriate to wear when attending a conference or competing at a business pitch conference makes all the difference. When students get to attend these events and are educated on the proper attire, they want to dress to fit the occasion. It makes them feel great when they are being treated like adults!

HOOKED Students

I never knew there was a way to dress business casual and business professional. I just thought there was business and non-business.

~ Jordan W.

It helped me get a vision on what I'll have to do when I get a job and what to expect.

~ Braelyn H.

UNLOCKING the Lesson: How to Dress Professionally

Overall society has become more casual when it come to dress code, but there are some professions and situations that require an understanding of business casual and business professional. Encourage students to know the difference and when each is appropriate.

The NUTS and BOLTS

- How to Dress Professionally lesson materials
- Old magazines
- Scissors
- Glue sticks

My CHAIN of Events

1. Review the "Professional Dress Tips and Trick" handout with your students.
2. Have students complete the "Business Dress Matching" worksheet using the tips and tricks from the handout.
3. Using old magazines or printouts from the internet, students cut out clothing items and accessories. They will then glue them in the proper section of the "Build Your Outfit" worksheet to build their perfect outfit for each category.

 **The GEARS Are Moving**

Use either the "Business Dress Matching" or the "Build Your Outfit" worksheet to evaluate if students used the tips and tricks in deciding on proper clothing for each situation.

 **KEY Hints**

- **Use celebrity outfits as examples.** Find images online of celebrity outfits and have students classify them as casual, business casual or business professional.

How to Count Back Change

A few years ago I thought it would be a good idea to have the student council volunteer to run the concession stand at one of the home football games. I am one of the staff sponsors for the group and I figured it would be a great way to raise some funds for our organization. Boy, was I in for a night!

None of these students had the confidence to make change for customers buying snacks. It's definitely not that they couldn't subtract seven dollars' worth of snacks from a 20-dollar bill, they just couldn't apply the math to actually count back the change to the customer.

This is a skill not only needed if you are in a position to give change to someone else, but for everyone who will ever receive change back from making a purchase. You want to make sure you are receiving the correct change back, right? After explaining this fact to students, they were on board learning the proper way to count back change.

 HOOKED Students

This is actually helpful for day-to-day life.

~ Jack L.

I enjoyed learning to count back change. If I get a job soon it will be helpful.

~ Alannah D.

 **UNLOCKING the Lesson: How to Count Back Change**

Whether you need to count back change to someone else or you make sure you are receiving the correct change, counting back change is an important skill to teach our students.

 The NUTS and BOLTS

- How to Count Back Change lesson materials
- Play money

 **My CHAIN of Events**

- Use the "How to Count Back Change" worksheet to work through each situation with your students. Use the play money to physically work through each situation.
- Have students team up and draw "change situations" cards. They will use the play money to make and count back the change in each of the situations they draw.

 **The GEARS Are Moving**

After practicing with partners, have students choose a "change situation" card and count back the change to you.

 **KEY Hints**

- **Have multiple play money kits on hand.** Students retain the skill much better when physically counting out the money. Have multiple kits of fake money on hand for students to use.

How to Write a Professional Email

One of my biggest pet peeves has to be the lack of emailing skills possessed by my students. For a generation that has some of the most technological knowledge they lack the basic skill of sending a coherent email.

Here is a list of some of the most frustrating email faux pas my students make.

- Putting the entire email message in the subject line.
- Not completing the subject line.
- Not updating their automatic signature. (I have seniors who still have a signature that says they are a freshman.)
- Not paying attention to the spelling and grammar suggestions.
- Using text lingo.
- Making demands.

I'm sure you have experienced some or all of these and more. Students are so used to having all their conversations through Snapchat, and they forget there is a proper time to string together a complete sentence and use magic words like please and thank you.

HOOKED Students

I will use these new tips every time I email my teachers.

~ Gage H.

I enjoyed learning how I should properly be writing emails to my teachers.

~ Autumn C.

 **UNLOCKING the Lesson: How to Write a Professional Email**

Prepare your students for any career by teaching them how to properly communicate through email.

 **The NUTS and BOLTS**

♦ How to Write a Professional Email lesson materials

 **My CHAIN of Events**

1. Go over the "How to Write a Professional Email" handout with students.
2. Walk the students through how to update the automatic signature in the settings.
3. Have students complete the email assignment provided in the "How to Write a Professional Email" handout.

 **The GEARS Are Moving**

As students send you their emails, evaluate their use of the tips from the "How to Write a Professional Email" handout.

 **KEY Hints**

♦ **Respond to each student.** Give feedback to each student on what they did well and what they can improve upon.

How to Make a Professional Phone Call

Have you ever had to talk to a teenager on the phone? IT. IS. TORTURE. During the summers I teach business classes for an online academy. One of the requirements for the online academy is to have an initial meeting with each student. Typically, I hold a virtual meeting for this requirement, but if students can't make those scheduled meetings they have to call me for their meeting requirement.

These phone calls typically go like this:

ME: "Hello this is Mrs. Johnson."

Super long pause.

Parent sitting next to a student who is on the other end of the phone call: "Tell her who you are!"

STUDENT: "Umm. I'm in your class."

This awkward exchange tends to go on for a few more minutes as I explain the details of the class. I then ask if they have any questions. This is quickly followed by "No," and a click because they have hung up.

With all the ways to communicate without talking, students have lost the art of talking on the phone. They will never know the pain of lying on the floor by the wall talking to your best friend because the cord doesn't stretch far enough to sit on the kitchen chair.

As students get older there will be more and more times they need to speak to someone over the phone and they are scared to do it. Making students comfortable speaking on the phone will give them a leg up when it comes to making a first impression when applying for a job.

 HOOKED Students

Making a phone call helped to get over my fear of talking to people over the phone.
~ Kenna H.

I feel like we all need to learn how to make a phone call.
~ Hailey B.

 **UNLOCKING the Lesson: How to Make a Professional Phone Call**

Stressing the fact that not everything can be said in a text, prepare students for the inevitable necessity of speaking on the phone.

 **The NUTS and BOLTS**

- How to Make a Professional Phone lesson materials
- Kids play phones (optional)

 My CHAIN of Events

1. Review the "Steps to Making a Professional Phone Call" handout with students.
2. Have students partner up and use the "Phone Call Practice Cards" to practice different phone call situations.
3. Assign students the "Phone Call Scavenger Hunt" worksheet as homework. Students will call local businesses and use the skills they have learned to answer the scavenger hunt questions.

The GEARS Are Moving

Perform one of the practice cards with students to evaluate their use of the phone call tips.

 **KEY Hints**

- **Use play phones for practice.** For fun, have a couple of children's play phones for students to use while using the practice cards.

How to Write a Check

While check writing is a dying art form, there are still times when a check is necessary. Usually when registering my kids for a sport or activity or buying some sort of fundraiser candle is when I get to show off this skill.

Writing a check and understanding a checking account is not a difficult task but can really make a student feel like they have control over a piece of their life. All our students either already have or will soon have a checking account. Let's make sure they are equipped to handle it.

I used to only cover these lessons in my accounting classes, but as time has gone on, I have found the value in covering this skill in ALL of my classes.

 HOOKED Students

> I enjoyed learning how to write a check. I've seen my parents do it, but I've never written one.
> ~ Addison O.

> I enjoyed writing a check because I think it is very beneficial for kids to learn how to do this life skill.
> ~ Bridget D.

 **UNLOCKING the Lesson: How to Write a Check**

Students move closer to "adulthood" as they learn the skill of check writing.

 **The NUTS and BOLTS**

- How to Write a Check lesson materials

 My CHAIN of Events

1. Use the "How to Write a Check" worksheet to go over the parts of a check with students.
2. Have students complete the "Writing Checks" worksheet.

 The GEARS Are Moving

Check students "Writing Checks" worksheet against the skills learned from the "How to Write a Check" worksheet.

 **KEY Hints**

- **Combine this lesson with the "How to Make Change" lesson.** After students write their checks, use fake money and have them "cash" their check and count out the money.

How to Give a Professional Handshake

One of the first things my Entrepreneurship students learn is how to give a proper handshake. We have many guest speakers and community partners visit our class, many of which will extend a hand to the students for a handshake. In some instances, this is the first time an adult has offered to shake their hand. They get nervous because this seems like a simple practice, but you don't know what you don't know. If you have never given a handshake, you most likely don't know the right way to do so.

This lesson can be a lot of fun and alleviate the stress when guests start coming into class. Plus, community members are very impressed when a student is the first to extend their hand for a handshake!

 ## HOOKED Students

I never realized there was a wrong way to shake someone's hand.

~ Jace N.

I liked learning how to interact with people in the world and doing things that we will need to do later in life.

~ Jeremiah H.

 ## UNLOCKING the Lesson: How to Give a Professional Hand

Make your students the most impressive and confident teenagers in the area by teaching them to initiate and give a handshake like any professional.

 ## The NUTS and BOLTS

- How to Give a Professional Handshake lesson materials

 ## My CHAIN of Events

1. Use the "Steps to a Professional Handshake" handout to teach your student the six steps to give a confident handshake.
2. Have students practice their handshake with classmates.

3. Give students the "Handshake Rate Sheet" and have them shake hands with five adults in the building throughout the day and get feedback on their new skill.

 The GEARS Are Moving

Review the students' "Handshake Rate Sheet" to see how they did with their new skill.

 **KEY Hints**

◆ **Give your colleagues a heads up.** Let the other teachers in the building know your students will be coming around initiating handshakes. This probably isn't normal behavior and we don't want everyone thinking the full moon has caused weird behavior.

How to Write a Thank You Note

Everyone loves getting a handwritten thank you note. From little kids to grandparents, receiving a thank you note can make your day. Receiving a thank you note makes you feel that someone was thinking of you and appreciated your efforts.

Writing thank you notes in a professional setting can make you stand out form others. If you receive help from someone, thank them. You will be more likely to get help again in the future should you need it. This practice is all a part of building your professional network. Students who can build their networks will be miles ahead of their peers as they start their college or professional careers.

 HOOKED Students

It felt good to write a thank you not to someone else.

~ Alyssa Y.

I enjoyed writing a thank you note. I believe it will mean a lot to the people who receive the notes.

~ Kaitlin K.

I have trouble writing thank you notes because I never know what to say. It gave me an opportunity to really think about it and put a lot of thought into it.

~ Angel G.

UNLOCKING the Lesson: How to Write a Thank You Note

Prevent the extinction of the art of the thank you note by teaching students how to write them and how good it feels to receive them.

The NUTS and BOLTS

- How to Write a Thank You Note lesson materials
- Blank thank you notes (optional)

My CHAIN of Events

1. Review the "Tips for Writing a Thank You Note" handout with students.
2. Use the "Writing a Thank You Note" worksheet or blank thank you notes to have students write a thank you note to their favorite teacher. Remind them to use the tips they learned as well as their best handwriting.

The GEARS Are Moving

Use the "Tips for Writing a Thank You Note" handout to see if students used the tips to write their notes.

KEY Hints

- **Use real thank you notes.** Provide students with blank thank you notes for the assignment and deliver them to the teacher each student wrote their note to.

How to Address an Envelope

During my first year of teaching, I was having students write thank you notes to a guest speaker who came the previous day. I wrote the mailing address on the board and gave each student a stamp for their envelope. What happened over the next ten minutes left me speechless. Envelopes were turned in with stamps placed upside down and in the wrong corner, and addresses were written at the very top or bottom of the envelope, sometimes in one long line. I even had one with the address written on the back of the envelope.

In a high school classroom, I never would have guessed I would have to teach students how to address an envelope. But after thinking, I realized these students probably had very little reason to send a letter. Technology has advanced, and what once was a common skill has become a sporadic need but still needed.

 HOOKED Students

This is something you need to know for life, and we actually got to send it to a veteran.
~ Lydia M.

I enjoyed learning how to address an envelope.
~ Jordan T.

 **UNLOCKING the Lesson: How to Address an Envelope**

Teach students how to properly address an envelope to help round out some of those adult skills.

 **The NUTS and BOLTS**

- How to Address an Envelope lesson materials

 My CHAIN of Events

1. Complete the "Addressing and Envelop" worksheet with students.
2. Walk through addressing an envelope in a few different situations (P.O. box, etc.)
3. Have students complete the "Addressing and Envelop Scavenger Hunt."

 The GEARS Are Moving

Using the lesson material, check to see if students followed the guidelines to addressing an envelope.

 **KEY Hints**

- **Combine this lesson with the "How to Write a Thank You Note" lesson.** Students can then mail their thank you notes to the recipient.

Professionalism Day

Several years ago, I decided to dedicate a day in all my business classes to "lost" skills. I came up with ten different stations for students to rotate through, exposing them to everyday skills they need no matter what profession they choose. Professionalism Day was born. It has only grown as the years pass. Now, almost every teacher in the career and technical education (CTE) department at my school rotates their students through the stations. We set everything up for a week and have teachers sign up for times to bring their class to the event.

You can use Professionalism Day as a culmination event after using all the professional skills lessons in this unit or use it by itself as a quick introduction to skills unfamiliar to students. Either way, this is always a fun event that will have students talking.

 HOOKED Students

Certain stations were things I've never been taught so it was nice to at least be introduced to a couple things.
~ Sophia G.

I enjoyed that I got to learn some things that I didn't already know that are useful in life.
~Allie J.

I enjoyed learning new things because I'm growing up and these are some things I need to know.
~McKayla R.

What I enjoyed most was the ironing and steaming a shirt because I never knew how easy it was. And it was just satisfying from watching it go from wrinkly to nonwrinkled.
~ Destiny L.

I think the thing I enjoyed the most about the professionalism day stations was the interactions with the other students and learning how to make a professionalism phone call, and tying a tie was really helpful.
~ Romalie T.

 **UNLOCKING the Lesson: Professionalism Day**

Professionalism Day Stations is a one class period, hands-on, activity-based lesson for students to be exposed to real-world skills needed for adulthood. Students rotate through ten different stations where they are taught and perform professional skills they may not have been exposed to but will need post high school.

**Stations should be set up around the room for students to visit freely. For a class of 25 it typically takes about an hour to complete all ten stations. I will break down materials and preparation by each station.*

How to Tie a Tie

 **The NUTS and BOLTS**

- Poster
- A variety of neckties
- Mirror (optional)

 My CHAIN of Events

1. Display the "How to Tie a Tie" poster and place ties and a mirror on a desk. (Students can use the mirror to watch themselves perfect their technique).
2. An adult in the room will sign off on the student worksheet once they have successfully tied their tie.

 **KEY Hints**

- **Get kookie ties.** Students really enjoy fun character ties.
- **Invite guests.** I invite some of our male administrators and guidance counselors to help give tips and sign off on worksheets as the students complete their ties.
- **Be ready for questions.** Female students sometimes ask why they need to learn this skill. My response is always, "You never know when the Avril Lavigne tie look will be back in style." (Most of the time I just get a blank stare back).

How to Iron or Steam a Shirt

 The NUTS and BOLTS

- Poster
- Multiple dress shirts, both men's and women's style

- Ironing board (I prefer the tabletop version)
- Irons
- Spray bottles
- Steamer
- Hangers
- Basket

My CHAIN of Events

1. Display the "How to Iron/Steam a Shirt" poster and set up the boards and irons.
2. Fill the spray bottles and steamer with water and make sure to turn the irons and steamers on before the students get to class.
3. An adult in the room will sign off on the student worksheet once they have ironed or steamed their shirt.

KEY Hints

- **Keep items wrinkled.** Make sure to wrinkle the shirts before the students arrive and have them in the basket. The more shirts you have, the better it would be, but if you run short do your best to wrinkle them between classes or students.
- **Invite adult guests.** Invite administrators and guidance counselors to help give tips and sign off on worksheets as the students complete their task.
- **Keep students from burning themselves.** It's always a great idea to remind the student that the iron and steam are hot.

How to Write a Check

The NUTS and BOLTS

- Poster
- Pens

My CHAIN of Events

1. Display the "How to Write a Check" poster and place pens on a desk.
2. Fill in the blanks on the poster for parts of a check: who to write the check to, how much the check should be for, and what the check is for (memo).
3. Students then fill out the check on their worksheet.

 KEY Hints

- **Change up the information.** If you are doing this lesson with more than one class, I suggest changing up the information for whom the students will be writing the check. It keeps the students on their toes.

How to Give a Professional Handshake

 **The NUTS and BOLTS**

- Poster

 My CHAIN of Events

1. Display the "How to Give a Professional Handshake" poster.
2. Students will work with a partner and follow the steps in the video to practice giving a professional handshake.
3. Students will record the name of their handshake partner on their worksheet.

 **KEY Hints**

- **Utilize your adult volunteers.** The administration and guidance counselors in the room make for good handshake partners.

How to Make Change

 The NUTS and BOLTS

- Poster
- Fake money

 My CHAIN of Events

1. Display the "How to Make Change" poster and place fake money on a desk.
2. Fill in the blanks on the poster. Students will use the story to determine how much change will be needed.
3. Students will work with a partner to follow the steps in the video to count back change.
4. Students will record the bills they used to make change on their worksheet.

 **KEY Hints**

- **Encourage students to walk through the steps a few times**. It may take a few times walking through the steps for students to get the hang of it.

How to Write a Professional Email

 The NUTS and BOLTS

- Poster
- Students will need a device to send the email.

 My CHAIN of Events

1. Display the "How to Write a Professional Email" poster.
2. Fill in the blanks on the poster for the details the students will need to send the email.

3. Students will use the tips from the video and the details from the poster to send you an email.

 **KEY Hints**

- **Answer each student's email.** Responding to each of the student emails with feedback on positives and how they can improve is very effective.

Social Media Etiquette

 The NUTS and BOLTS

- Poster

 My CHAIN of Events

1. Display the "Social Media Etiquette" poster.
2. Students will use the tips from the video to pick appropriate social media posts for a professional and record a response on their worksheet.

 **KEY Hints**

- **Find examples of what not to do.** Giving celebrity faux pas can be a lighthearted way to cover some of the "things not to do."

How to Make a Professional Phone Call

 **The NUTS and BOLTS**

- Poster
- Classroom phone
- Teacher or staff member in another room to answer student calls

My CHAIN of Events

1. Display the "How to Make a Professional Phone Call" poster.
2. Fill in the blanks on the poster.
3. Create a list of students with assigned "interview times" and give it to the teacher/staff member in another room answering the calls.
4. Students use tips from the video and the script to set up an "interview time" (the other teacher will give the students their designated "interview time" to fill out on their worksheet).

 KEY Hints

♦ **Update your volunteers.** Let the adult on the other end know when everyone has completed this station, so they aren't waiting for more calls.

How to Write a Thank You Note

The NUTS and BOLTS

♦ Poster
♦ Pens
♦ Thank you notes

My CHAIN of Events

1. Display the "How to Write a Thank You Note" poster and put the pens and thank you notes on a desk.
2. Fill in the blanks on the poster for whom students will be writing their notes.
3. Students will use tips from the video to write their thank you note.

 **KEY Hints**

♦ **Find a local veterans' organization to team up with.** Have students write their notes to thank a veteran and send them to the organization. We send our thank you notes to the Honor Flight organization that flies veterans to Washington, DC. They receive their notes while on the flight.

How to Address an Envelope

 **The NUTS and BOLTS**

♦ Poster
♦ Pens
♦ Paperclips
♦ Stickers that look like stamps

 My CHAIN of Events

1. Display the "How to Address an Envelope" poster and put pens, stickers, and paper clips on a desk.
2. Fill in the blanks on the poster with the address and return address the student will use.
3. Students will use the tips from the video and address the envelope of the thank you note they wrote from that station.
4. Students will paperclip the thank you note and envelope to their worksheet.

 KEY Hints

♦ **Use the school's address as the return address.** Have the student address the envelope with the school's address as

the return address and the veteran's organization address as the mailing address.
- **Check the notes before you send them.** Don't have students seal the envelope so you can check their notes before they are sent.
- **Combine notes in one big envelope.** Put all the thank you notes in one big envelope to mail to the organization (remember the "stamps" on the student envelopes are only stickers).

 The GEARS Are Moving

The station's worksheet is designed to be graded if you choose to record a grade for the activity. When students complete all ten stations, distribute Professionalism Day Certificates to students. Take pictures and share on the school's social media accounts!

Social Media Etiquette

SOCIAL MEDIA ETIQUETTE

KEEP IT POSITIVE!

Don't overuse hashtags.

DON'T POST PHOTOS YOU WOULDN'T WANT YOUR GRANDMA TO SEE.

Don't post too frequently.

DON'T OVERSHARE PERSONAL INFORMATION.

Don't speak badly about your place of employment.

Social Media Etiquette Card Sort

Cut out the social media post cards below and sort them into two categories; **Appropriate** and **Not Appropriate**.

A photo of you on vacation with details including; where you are and how long you will be there.	A complaint about your boss because she made you work three weekends in a row.	A photo of your dog after being groomed with a caption, "Cutest dog in all the land!"
A photo of you at a party making inappropriate hand gestures.	A photo of the sunset with the caption, "Beautiful!"	A motivational quote with a link to an article on leadership.
Several posts in one day about a pie you baked.	A gloomy post about how you hate your life and everyone in it.	A post about how you hate when people tell you what to do.
A post that states, "Living the Good Life." #Living #Good #LovingLife #Awesome #GreatLife	A post about how busy you are with a list of everything you are doing that day.	A post about what you are thankful for.

Name _____ Period ____ Date_____

Social Media Etiquette Card Sort Reflection

Explain why you categorized each social media post as "Not Appropriate" or "Appropriate."

Not Appropriate

Appropriate

How to Dress Professionally

Copyright material from Ashley Johnson, *Unlocking the Career and Technical Education Classroom*, 2025, Routledge

PROFESSIONAL DRESS TIPS AND TRICKS

Business Casual

DOS
- Button up Shirts
- Polo Shirts
- Blouse
- Khaki Pants
- Dark Jeans
- Knee Length
- Maxi Dresses
- Closed Toe Shoes

DON'TS
- Shorts
- Flip Flops
- Pants with Holes
- T-Shirts
- Sweatpants/Shirts
- Tank Tops
- Crop Tops
- Too Tight/Loose Clothes

Business Professional

DOS
- Blazers/Jackets
- Suits
- Ties
- Minimal Jewlery
- Loafers
- Pumps

DON'TS
- Jeans
- Tennis Shoes
- Bulky Jewlery
- Skirts Above the Knee
- Polos
- Open Toed Shoes

Name _____ Period ____ Date_____

Business Dress Matching

Match the business situation with the appropriate dress.

1. You and some colleagues are going to a seminar outside of the office. The dress code is business casual. What do you wear?

Khaki Pants		T-Shirt		Pant Suit
Polo Shirt	OR	Shorts	OR	Blouse
Loafers		Flip Flops		Pumps

2. You are giving a big presentation to potential clients. Your boss wants you to dress business professional. What do you wear?

Khaki Pants		T-Shirt		Pant Suit
Polo Shirt	OR	Shorts	OR	Blouse
Loafers		Flip Flops		Pumps

3. You are going to the beach with some friends. What do you wear?

Khaki Pants		T-Shirt		Pant Suit
Polo Shirt	OR	Shorts	OR	Blouse
Loafers		Flip Flops		Pumps

Describe what you would wear.

You are interviewing for a part-time job at an local office supply store to make some money while you go to college. Describe what you would wear to this interview.

_____
_____
_____

Name _____ Period ____ Date_____

Build Your Outfit

Using old magazines or printouts from the internet, have students build their own outfit for each category below. Make sure to include shoes and accessories.

Casual

Business Casual

Business Professional

How to Count Back Change

Name _____ Period ____ Date_____

How to Count Back Change

Walk through the steps to count back change in each of the situations.

Steps to Count Back Change:
1. Start by using pennies to complete the cents to the nearest 5 or 10 cents.
2. Next, use nickels or dimes to get your cents to the nearest quarter dollar.
3. Use quarters to reach your nearest dollar.
4. Use one dollar bills to reach your nearest five or ten multiple.
5. Use five or ten dollar bills to reach your next twenty multiple.
6. Use twenty dollar bills to reach your next one hundred multiple.

<u>EXAMPLE</u>:
You are working at a snack bar. A customer's total order comes to $42.36. She hands you a $100 bill. You need to count back the customer's change.
1. Use **4 pennies** to reach $42.40.
2. Use **1 dime** to reach $42.50.
3. Use **2 quarters** to reach $43.00.
4. Use **2 one dollar bills** to reach $45.00.
5. Use **1 five dollar bill** to reach $50.00.
6. Use **1 ten dollar bill** to reach $60.00.
7. Use **2 twenty dollar bills** to reach $100.00.

The customer receives ***$57.64 in change***.

<u>Situation 1</u>:
You are working at a snack bar. A customer's total order comes to $57.12. She hands you a $100 bill. You need to count back the customer's change.
1. Use _____ **pennies** to reach $_____ .
2. Use _____ **dime** to reach $_____ .
3. Use _____ **quarters** to reach $_____ .
4. Use _____ **one dollar bills** to reach $_____ .
5. Use _____ **five dollar bill** to reach $_____ .
6. Use _____ **ten dollar bill** to reach $_____ .
7. Use _____ **twenty dollar bills** to reach $_____ .

The customer receives **$_____ in change**.

Situation 2:
You are working at a snack bar. A customer's total order comes to $24.59. She hands you a $100 bill. You need to count back the customer's change.
1. Use _____ **pennies** to reach $_____ .
2. Use _____ **dime** to reach $_____ .
3. Use _____ **quarters** to reach $_____ .
4. Use _____ **one dollar bills** to reach $_____ .
5. Use _____ **five dollar bill** to reach $_____ .
6. Use _____ **ten dollar bill** to reach $_____ .
7. Use _____ **twenty dollar bills** to reach $_____ .

The customer receives $_____ **in change**.

Situation 3:
You are working at a snack bar. A customer's total order comes to $31.23. She hands you a $100 bill. You need to count back the customer's change.
1. Use _____ **pennies** to reach $_____ .
2. Use _____ **dime** to reach $_____ .
3. Use _____ **quarters** to reach $_____ .
4. Use _____ **one dollar bills** to reach $_____ .
5. Use _____ **five dollar bill** to reach $_____ .
6. Use _____ **ten dollar bill** to reach $_____ .
7. Use _____ **twenty dollar bills** to reach $_____ .

The customer receives $_____ **in change**.

Situation 4:
You are working at a snack bar. A customer's total order comes to $63.28. She hands you a $100 bill. You need to count back the customer's change.
1. Use _____ **pennies** to reach $_____ .
2. Use _____ **dime** to reach $_____ .
3. Use _____ **quarters** to reach $_____ .
4. Use _____ **one dollar bills** to reach $_____ .
5. Use _____ **five dollar bill** to reach $_____ .
6. Use _____ **ten dollar bill** to reach $_____ .
7. Use _____ **twenty dollar bills** to reach $_____ .

The customer receives $_____ **in change**.

Change Situation

You owe $35.76.
You pay with a $50 bill.

Change Situation

You owe $12.43.
You pay with a $20 bill.

Change Situation

You owe $47.32.
You pay with a $100 bill.

Change Situation

You owe $5.56.
You pay with a $10 bill.

Change Situation

You owe $77.45.
You pay with a $100 bill.

Change Situation

You owe $2.31.
You pay with a $5 bill.

Change Situation

You owe $34.66.
You pay with two $20 bills.

Change Situation

You owe $58.96.
You pay with three $20 bills.

Change Situation

You owe $11.24.
You pay with a $50 bill.

Change Situation

You owe $17.32.
You pay with a $50 bill.

Change Situation

You owe $54.37.
You pay with a $100 bill.

Change Situation

You owe $6.44.
You pay with a $10 bill.

Change Situation

You owe $73.15.
You pay with four $20 bills.

Change Situation

You owe $13.21.
You pay with a $50 bill.

Change Situation

You owe $18.45.
You pay with two $10 bills.

Change Situation

You owe $23.12.
You pay with a $20 and a $5 bill.

How to Write a Professional Email

Name _____ Period ____ Date_____

How to Write a Professional Email

Steps to Writing a Professional Email:

1. **Subject Line:** Make sure you fill out the subject line to include a short phrase that summarizes what the email is about.
2. **Greeting:** Include a short greeting using the name of the person to whom you are writing the email.
3. **Message:** Craft a short message that gets to the point. Use complete sentences with correct capitalization and punctuation.
4. **Signature:** Make sure you have your automatic signature up-to-date in settings so it automatically populates in the email.

EXAMPLE:
Subject Line: Thursday's Marketing Meeting

Good Morning Susan,

I wanted to remind you about Thursday's marketing meeting in the conference room. Please bring your ideas for the new campaign. Lunch will be provided.

Jane Douglas
DIrector of Marketing
jdouglas@email.com
(123)456-7890

Your Turn:

Send an email to your teacher. You need to schedule a time to take a make-up test because you were absent from school last Friday.

How to Make a Professional Phone Call

Steps to Making a Professional Phone Call

 **1. IDENTIFY YOURSELF.**

2. ASK HOW THE OTHER PERSON'S DAY IS GOING.

 **3. STATE THE REASON FOR THE CALL.**

4. REPEAT THE DETAILS TO MAKE SURE YOU HEARD CORRECTLY.

 **5. WISH THEM A GREAT DAY!**

Phone Call Practice Card

Scheduling an Interview

Hello, my name is _____.
How is your day going?

I would like to set up an interview time for the student assistant position.

Okay, thank you, I will see you at ____ o'clock on _____.

Have a great day!

Phone Call Practice Card

Pizza Shop

Hello, my name is _____.
How is your day going?

Can you tell me how much it cost for a large, one-topping pizza?

Okay, so that is $_____ for a large, one-topping pizza?

Have a great day!

Phone Call Practice Card

Auto Center

Hello, my name is _____.
How is your day going?

How much does it cost for a basic oil change?

Okay, so that is $_____.?

Have a great day!

Phone Call Practice Card

Post Office

Hello, my name is _____.
How is your day going?

Can you please tell me your Saturday office hours?

Okay, so that is ___ to ___?

Have a great day!

Phone Call Practice Card

Chamber of Commerce

Hello, my name is _____.
How is your day going?

Can you tell me how much it cost for a business to become a chamber member?

Okay, so that is $_____?

Have a great day!

Phone Call Practice Card

Local Bank

Hello, my name is _____.
How is your day going?

Can you tell me how much is needed to deposit to open a basic checking account?

Okay, so that is $_____?

Have a great day!

Phone Call Practice Card

Dry Cleaner

Hello, my name is _____.
How is your day going?

How much does it cost to clean a King-sized comforter?

Okay, so that is $_____?

Have a great day!

Phone Call Practice Card

Employment Inquiry

Hello, my name is _____.
How is your day going?

Are you currently hiring?

How should I apply for a position?

Ok, so I will _____?

Have a great day!

Name _____ Period _____ Date _____

Phone Call Scavenger Hunt

Find the phone number of a local business for each category, call and obtain the information requested.

LOCAL PIZZA SHOP
How much does a large, one topping pizza cost?
_____

LOCAL AUTO CENTER
How much does an oil change cost?
_____

POST OFFICE
What are their Saturday hours?
_____

CHAMBER OF COMMERCE
How much does it cost to be a chamber member?
_____

LOCAL BANK
How much money do you need to open a basic savings account?
_____

LOCAL DRY CLEANER
How much does it cost to clean a King-sized comforter?
_____

How to Write a Check

Betty Miller
123 Main Street
Big City, TX 75032

2024

Date: _____

Pay to the order of _____ $ _____

_____

Memo _____ _____

⑂4678845⑂ 788520 2024

Name _____ Period ____ Date_____

How to Write a Check

With every checking account, you have the ability to write checks. While a debit card can be used most of the time, there are instances when you need to write a check.

Checks consist of the following elements:
1. **Check Number:** Each check has a unique check number.
2. **Account Owner Information:** The name and address of the checking account owner.
3. **Date Line:** The date the check was written.
4. **Payee Line:** The name of the person or business to whom you are writing the check.
5. **Dollar Box:** The amount the check is written for in numerical form.
6. **Amount of Check:** The amount the check is written for in words.
7. **Memo Line:** A description of what you are paying for.
8. **Signature Line:** Account holder signs the check here.
9. **Routing Number:** A specific number assigned to each bank.
10. **Account number:** The account number for the checking account.

Example:

Write check number 2024 to Amy Buster for $50.25 for flowers from a fundraiser. The date is October 1st of the current year.

Name _____ Period ____ Date_____

Writing Checks

Use the information for each situation to fill out the check.

#1
Write check number 101 to your favorite restaurant for $75.16 for dinner. The date is May 1st of the current year.

```
YOUR NAME
123 Main Street
Big City, TX 75032                                    101

                                        Date: _____

Pay to the
order of _____  $ _____

_____

🏛
Memo _____   _____
  ⑆4678845⑆ 788520  101
```

#2
Write check number 102 to one of your classmates for $100 for a concert ticket. The date is April 21st of the current year.

```
YOUR NAME
123 Main Street
Big City, TX 75032                                    102

                                        Date: _____

Pay to the
order of _____  $ _____

_____

🏛
Memo _____   _____
  ⑆4678845⑆ 788520  102
```

#3
Write check number 103 to your school for $35 for a sweatshirt. The date is September 11th of the current year.

```
YOUR NAME
123 Main Street
Big City, TX 75032                                    103

                                        Date: _____

Pay to the
order of _____  $ _____

_____

🏛
Memo _____   _____
  ⑆4678845⑆ 788520  103
```

Copyright material from Ashley Johnson, *Unlocking the Career and Technical Education Classroom*, 2025, Routledge

How to Give a Professional Handshake

STEPS TO A PROFESSIONAL HANDSHAKE

 **1** Stand with your body square to the other person.

 **2** Offer your hand.

3 Grip firmly with palm-to-palm contact.

 **4** Make eye contact and smile.

 **5** Give two firm pumps.

 **6** Release while starting your conversation.

Name _____ Period ____ Date_____

Handshake Rate Sheet

Find five adults to shake hands with throughout the day. Have them rate your handshake on a scale of 1-10 (10 being the best) and give suggestions for improvement.

Name: _____

1---2---3---4---5---6---7---8---9---10

Handshake suggestions:

Name: _____

1---2---3---4---5---6---7---8---9---10

Handshake suggestions:

Name: _____

1---2---3---4---5---6---7---8---9---10

Handshake suggestions:

Name: _____

1---2---3---4---5---6---7---8---9---10

Handshake suggestions:

Name: _____

1---2---3---4---5---6---7---8---9---10

Handshake suggestions:

Copyright material from Ashley Johnson, *Unlocking the Career and Technical Education Classroom*, 2025, Routledge

How to Write a Thank You Note

Copyright material from Ashley Johnson, *Unlocking the Career and Technical Education Classroom*, 2025, Routledge

TIPS FOR WRITING A THANK YOU NOTE

1. Address the recipient using "Dear" and his/her name.

2. Express your gratitude!

3. Mention specific details.

4. Repeat your thanks.

5. Add a closing (sincerely, regards, etc.) and signature.

EXAMPLE:
Dear Thomas,

Thank you so much for your donation to our silent auction. The candle basket will be a hit. All the money we raise will go toward new uniforms for the band. It's because of donations from people like you, that we will be able to fund our program. Thank you again!

With Appreciation,

Sally Jensen

Name _____ Period ____ Date _____

Write a Thank You Note

Below, write a thank you note to a teacher. Make sure to follow the tips for writing a thank you note!

Copyright material from Ashley Johnson, *Unlocking the Career and Technical Education Classroom*, 2025, Routledge

How to Address an Envelop

Name _____ Period ____ Date_____

Addressing an Envelope

Addressing an envelope consists of **THREE** main parts; the mailing address, the return address, and the stamp.

- The **mailing address** is the address of the recipient of the letter and consists of; the name of the recipient, street number and name, city, state, and zip code. The mailing address appears on the center of the envelope.
- The **return address** is your mailing address including; your name, street number and name, city, state, and zip code. The return address appears in the upper left hand corner of the envelope.
- The **stamp** is the payment to mail the letter. The stamp appears in the upper right hand corner of the envelope.

```
┌─────────────────────────────────────────────────┐
│  Roger Rutger      Return                 [🌸]  │
│  987 First Street  Address               Stamp  │
│  Springfield, MO 65619                          │
│                                                 │
│              Mailing  Betty Sue Butler          │
│              Address  123 Main Street           │
│                       Springfield, IL 62629     │
└─────────────────────────────────────────────────┘
```

Give It A Try!
Using your name and the school's address as the return address, address the envelope below to Mark Melburn. Mark's mailing address is 456 South Benson Street, Big City, OH 45678. Draw a stamp in the proper location.

```
┌─────────────────────────────────────────────────┐
│                                                 │
│                                                 │
│                                                 │
│                                                 │
│                                                 │
│                                                 │
│                                                 │
└─────────────────────────────────────────────────┘
```

Addressing an Envelope to a P.O. Box

P.O. Box stands for **Post Office Box**. When addressing a letter to a recipient who has a P.O. Box, you simply need; the recipient's address, the P.O. Box number, and the city, state, and zip code. The letter will them be placed in the proper box at the post office in the specified city for the recipient to pick up.

Addressing an Envelope to Business with a Specific Recipient

When addressing an envelope to a specific person at a place of business you will include; the business name, an attention line with the recipient's name, the street address, city, state and zip code.

Give It A Try!

Using your name and the school's address as the return address, address the envelope below to Mark Melburn. Mark has a P.O. Box, #790 and lives in, Big City, OH 45678. Draw a stamp in the proper location.

Using your name and the school's address as the return address, address the envelope below to Mark Melburn. Mark works at Venture Capital Corporation and the address is 235 Startup Road, Big City, OH 45678. Draw a stamp in the proper location.

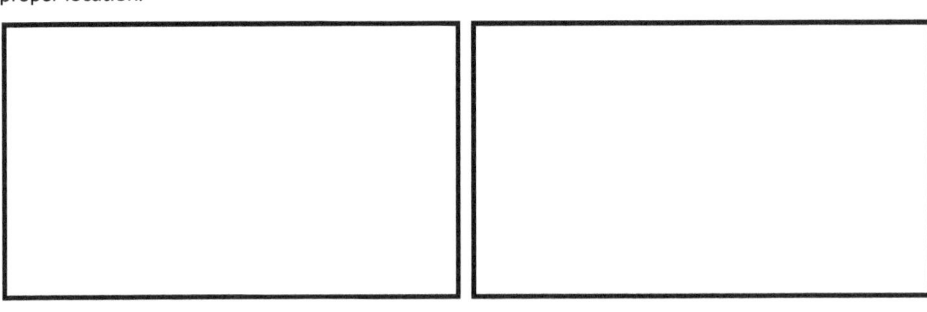

Name _____ Period _____ Date _____

Addressing an Envelope Scavenger Hunt

For each of the situations below, search the internet to find the proper address and recipient (if applicable). Us this information to address the envelope. Use your name and the school's address as the return address, and draw a stamp in the proper location.

#1
Address this envelope to the executive director of your local chamber of commerce.

#2
Address this envelope to the Fire Chief of your local Fire Department.

#3
Address this envelope to the Mayor of your town.

#4
Address this envelope to the CEO of the Coca-Cola Company.

#5
Address this envelope to the owner of your favorite sports team.

#6
Address this envelope to the manager of your nearest Wal-Mart.

#7
Address this envelope to your best friend.

Name: _____ Date _____ Period _____

Student Worksheet

Rotate through today's stations. For each station, watch the instructional video, complete the instructed skill, then fill out any needed information. When you complete all stations, turn this worksheet into your teacher.

Social Media Etiquette:

A.

A photo of the sunset with the caption, "Beautiful!"

B.

A complaint about your boss because she made you work three weekends in a row.

C.

Several posts in one day about a pie you baked.

Which of the social media posts above would be considered "not appropriate"? Explain.

How to Tie a Tie:

Have a monitor sign off when you have successfully tied your tie.

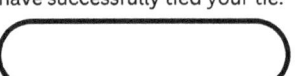

How to Iron/Steam a Shirt:

Have a monitor sign off when you have successfully ironed/steamed your shirt.

How to Write a Professional Email:

Once you have sent your email, put a check mark in the box below.

How to Write a Thank You Note:
How to Address an Envelope:

After you write your thank you note and address the envelope, paperclip it to this worksheet. Do not seal the envelope.

Copyright material from Ashley Johnson, *Unlocking the Career and Technical Education Classroom*, 2025, Routledge

How to Write a Check:

Using the information on the poster, fill out the check below.

```
YOUR NAME                                              1234
123 Main Street
Big City, TX 75032
                                    Date: _____

Pay to the
order of _____ $ [      ]

_____

🏛
Memo _____            _____
⑆4678845⑆ 788520  1234
```

How to Count Back Change:

Using the situations on the poster, determine the bills and coins that should be given to the customer for their change.

Situation 1:
Total Change Owed: _____
Breakdown:

Pennies	Ones
Nickels	Fives
Dimes	Tens
Quarters	Twentys

Situation 2:
Total Change Owed: _____
Breakdown:

Pennies	Ones
Nickels	Fives
Dimes	Tens
Quarters	Twentys

How to Give a Professional Handshake:

Have your partner sign in the box below.

How to Make a Professional Phone Call:

What day and time is your interview?

Social Media Etiquette

https://bit.ly/3ZELHq7

Steps to Social Media Etiquette:
1. Keep it positive.
2. Don't overshare personal information.
3. Don't overuse hashtags.
4. Don't post too frequently.
5. Don't post photos you wouldn't want your grandma to see.
6. Don't speak badly about your place of employment.

EXAMPLE:

| A motivational quote with a link to an article on leadership. | Too much personal information | A photo of you on vacation with details including; where you are and how long you will be there. |

Task:
Using the social media tips, determine which social media posts on the worksheet would be considered appropriate.

How to Iron or Steam a Shirt

https://bit.ly/4dpGfdX

Steps to Iron a Shirt:
1. **Collar:** If able, unbutton the shirt and lay the collar flat on the board. Spray the collar and iron.
2. **Sleeves:** Lay a sleeve flat on the board, spray and iron.
3. **Front:** Lay the front (one side at a time) on the board, spay and iron.
4. **Back:** Lay the back on the board, spray and iron.

Steps to Steam a Shirt:
1. Hang shirt on a hanger and hang from a door.
2. After steamer heats up, hold fabric tight while keeping the steamer about an inch from the shirt.
3. Repeat until you have steamed the entire garment.

Task:
Using one of the shirts provided, practice ironing or steaming. Have your worksheet signed by a monitor when the task is complete.

How to Tie a Tie

https://bit.ly/3THRV4A

Steps to Tie a Tie:
1. Start with the thick end on your right side.
2. The skinny side should be about 12 inches shorter than the thick side.
3. Take the thick side over the skinny side to the left and around.
4. Bring the thick side up into the neck loop from underneath.
5. Bring the thick side down through the loop you just made.
6. Tighten by pulling down on the thick end and pushing up on the knot.

Task:
Practice using one of the ties provided. Have your worksheet signed by a monitor when the task is complete.

How to Count Back Change

https://bit.ly/3Bkeia9

Steps to Count Back Change:
1. Start by using pennies to complete the cents to the nearest 5 or 10 cents.
2. Next, use nickels or dimes to get your cents to the nearest quarter dollar.
3. Use quarters to reach your nearest dollar.
4. Use one dollar bills to reach your nearest five or ten multiple.
5. Use five or ten dollar bills to reach your next twenty multiple.
6. Use twenty dollar bills to reach your next one hundred multiple.

<u>EXAMPLE</u>:

You are working at a snack bar. A customer's total order comes to $42.36. She hands you a $100 bill. You need to count back the customer's change.
1. Use **4 pennies** to reach $42.40.
2. Use **1 dime** to reach $42.50.
3. Use **2 quarters** to reach $43.00.
4. Use **2 one dollar bills** to reach $45.00.
5. Use **1 five dollar bill** to reach $50.00.
6. Use **1 ten dollar bill** to reach $60.00.
7. Use **2 twenty dollar bills** to reach $100.00.

The customer receives ***$57.64 in change***.

Task:
1. Your next customer at the snack bar has an order that comes to $_____. He hands you a $_____ bill. Count back the change with your partner then record the coins and bills used on your worksheet.
2. Your next customer at the snack bar has an order that comes to $_____. She hands you a $_____ bill. Count back the change with your partner then record the coins and bills used on your worksheet.

How to Write a Professional Email

https://bit.ly/3THwRLI

Steps to Writing a Professional Email:
1. **Subject Line:** Make sure you fill out the subject line to include a short phrase that summarizes what the email is about.
2. **Greeting:** Include a short greeting using the name of the person to whom you are writing the email.
3. **Message:** Craft a short message that gets to the point. Use complete sentences with correct capitalization and punctuation.
4. **Signature:** Make sure you have your automatic signature set up in settings so it automatically populates in the email.

EXAMPLE:
Subject Line: Thursday's Marketing Meeting

Good Morning Susan,

I wanted to remind you about Thursday's marketing meeting in the conference room. Please bring your ideas for the new campaign. Lunch will be provided.

Jane Douglas
DIrector of Marketing
jdouglas@email.com
(123)456-7890

Task:
Send an email to _____ asking to set up a time to meet an talk about the Science lab you missed last week.

Copyright material from Ashley Johnson, *Unlocking the Career and Technical Education Classroom*, 2025, Routledge

How to Make a Professional Phone Call

https://bit.ly/4dlqSTC

Steps to Making a Professional Phone Call:

1. Identify yourself.
2. Ask how the other person's day is going.
3. State the reason for the call.
4. Repeat back the details to make sure you heard them correctly.
5. Wish them a great day!

<u>EXAMPLE</u>:
Hello, can I speak with Mr. Ford?
How is your day going?
My name is _____ and I would like to set up an interview time for the student assistant position.
Okay, thank you, I will see you at ____ o'clock on _____.
Have a great day!

Task:

Call _____ at extension _____ to set up a time for an interview . Write down the day and time of the interview on your worksheet.

How to Write a Check

https://bit.ly/3Bv692s

Steps to Writing a Check:
1. **Date:** Write the date in the upper right hand corner.
2. **Pay to the Order Of:** The name of the person or organization you are writing the check to goes on this line.
3. **Amount:** In numerical form, write the amount of the check in the box next to the "pay to the order of" line.
4. **Amount (again):** The line under the "pay to the order of" line is for the amount of the check to be written in words with the change out of 100.
5. **Memo:** In the lower left hand corner, on the memo line, write what the check is for.
6. **Signature:** On the line in the lower right hand corner, sign your name.

EXAMPLE:

	2023
	Date: September 8, 2023
Pay to the order of Peter Buddington	$ 123.45
One hundred twenty-three and 45/100 --------------------------	
Memo____Vacation____	Beth Bontrager
4678845 788520 2023	

Task:

On your worksheet, write a check using today's date for the amount of _____ for _____. Make the check out to _____.

Copyright material from Ashley Johnson, *Unlocking the Career and Technical Education Classroom*, 2025, Routledge

How to Give a Professional Handshake

https://bit.ly/3zALlGo

Steps to a Professional Handshake:

 Stand with your body square to the other person.

 Offer your hand.

3 Grip firmly with palm-to-palm contact.

 Make eye contact and smile.

 Give two firm pumps.

 Release while starting your conversation.

Task:

Practice giving a professional handshake with a partner. Have your partner sign your worksheet.

How to Write a Thank You Note

https://bit.ly/4drfHc5

Steps to Writing a Thank You Note:
1. Address the recipient using "Dear" and his/her name
2. Express your gratitude.
3. Mention some specific details.
4. Repeat your thanks.
5. Add a closing (sincerely, regards, etc.) and signature.

EXAMPLE:
Dear Thomas,

Thank you so much for your donation to our silent auction. The candle basket will be a hit. All the money we raise will go toward new uniforms for the band. It's because of donations from people like you, that we will be able to fund our program. Thank you again!

With Appreciation,

Sally Jensen

Task:

Write a thank you note to _____

thanking them for _____.

How to Address an Envelope

https://bit.ly/3MXaaiX

Steps to Address an Envelope:

1. Write the return address in the upper left hand corner with your name on the first line, the street address on the second line, and the city, state, and zip code on the third line.
2. Write the name and address of the person you are sending the letter to in the middle of the envelope with the receiver's name on the first line, the street address on the second line, and the city, state and zip code on the third line.
3. Place the stamp in the upper right hand corner.

EXAMPLE:

```
Martin Johnson
123 Main Street
Westville, IN 46788

                    Gabriel Hernandez
                    456 First Avenue
                    Butler, OH 58743
```

Task:

Address the envelope of your thank you note.

Use a sticker as your stamp.

Use the following as your return address: **Use the following as the send to address:**

_____   _____
_____   _____
_____   _____

Copyright material from Ashley Johnson, *Unlocking the Career and Technical Education Classroom*, 2025, Routledge

Professional Phone Call Student Interview Days and Times

Student Name	Assigned Interview Day	Assigned Interview Time
	Monday	9am
	Tuesday	10am
	Wednesday	11am
	Thursday	12 noon
	Friday	1pm
	Monday	2pm
	Tuesday	3pm
	Wednesday	4pm
	Thursday	9:30am
	Friday	10:30am
	Monday	11:30am
	Tuesday	1:30pm
	Wednesday	2:30pm
	Thursday	3:30pm
	Friday	4:30pm

CERTIFICATE
OF ACHIEVEMENT

PROUDLY PRESENTED TO:

For successfully completing Professionalism Day!

PROFESSIONALISM DAY

5
Digital Career Portfolio Unit

Jumping into the Work-Based Learning Coordinator role about ten years into my teaching career was new and exciting. Students in this program spent most of their time at their worksite learning on-the-job skills. They got to leave school for this (which was the main selling point of the program). However, they did have to meet with me for classroom instruction from time to time. This was not their favorite thing as they would rather be at their jobs.

The first year, I created many different lessons that involved professionalism, workplace conflict resolution, soft skills, and paycheck deductions. This is all great information they needed to know, but they moaned and groaned because they didn't recognize the real-world value. When they are at their job, they are in the real world and that's where they wanted to be.

The second year, I created a larger project I felt would meet their need for "relevancy": the Digital Career Portfolio. We spent a good deal of our class time together developing digital portfolios they could take with them once they graduated and use them to get a job. Students created these portfolios using a free website design tool so they could continue to update and use their work for years to come. Students seemed to feel this project was a much better use of their time because their drive to complete it was greater than past assignments and they whined a lot less.

You can pick and choose from these lessons to use with your students or use all of them and create the full digital career portfolio (rubric included). Either way, your students will be building their employability skills.

Personal Narrative

Student have probably been introduced to personal narratives in their English classes. Many will not understand and will even push back when you introduce the idea of a personal narrative being included with assignments like resumes and cover letters.

Personal narratives, when written with the idea of a person's values at the center, is the perfect addition to a resume or digital portfolio. This piece can be the deciding factor between two potential employees. Resumes and cover letters typically are straight facts, skills, and accomplishments. You can't tell a person's heart and values from these documents. Including a personal narrative with your resume package displays passion and sets your students apart from the pack.

 HOOKED Students

> I never thought about how values can change as you get older.
>
> ~Teegan I.

> I like that the personal narrative makes my portfolio truly me.
>
> ~Carter N.

 **UNLOCKING the Lesson: Personal Narrative**

Have students evaluate their values and incorporate those values into a personal narrative that can serve as the landing page of their digital portfolio.

 **The NUTS and BOLTS**

- Values Activity Cards
- Values Activity Worksheet
- Personal Narrative Template

 My CHAIN of Events

1. *Values Activity:* Print and cut out the "Values Activities" Cards. Give each student a set of cards, and do the following:

    A. Ask students to put the cards in order of what they value the most, the top being the most valued and the bottom being the least. Emphasize the fact there are no right or wrong answers.
    B. Have students share their top values and why.
    C. Ask the students to arrange their cards again, but this time give them the following situation: "You are 35 years old wanting to build a new house in the country for you, your spouse and two kids." Have students discuss if any of their values changed because of the situation given?
    D. One more time have students arrange their cards but give them the following situation: "You just won the lottery and now have $125 million dollars." Have students discuss if any of their values changed because of the situation given?
    E. Have students complete the reflection worksheet.

2. *Personal Narrative Template*: Print and have students complete the "Personal Narrative Template." They will then use the template to write their three-paragraph personal narrative as to why and what inspired them to choose the career path, they are interested in utilizing what they learned about their values from the activity. Students should include a photo in this section on their portfolio website.

 **The GEARS Are Moving**

Use the personal narrative section of the digital career portfolio rubric to evaluate students' final personal narratives.

 KEY Hints

- **Encourage students to lean into their values.** This piece of the digital portfolio is where students can really show their values and passions.
- **Team up with an English teacher.** An English teacher may be able to help with formatting. Maybe this assignment could count for both your class and English class?!?!

Resume

Typically, students know what a resume is and why they need one. But have you ever looked at the resumes students put together? I have seen my fair share of student created resumes that are less than desirable.

Many times, students are confused about what should be included and what order to put their information. The big issue though is formatting the document so it is appealing to the eye. I have seen resumes that are a single paragraph that takes up a quarter of a page; have inconsistent formatting when it comes to bullets, underlining, and spacing; and spelling and punctuation mistakes that will make your skin crawl.

Getting students to understand that employers spend about 30 seconds or less looking at a resume is the most important part of a resume lesson. Creating an attractive document that is easy to ready is incredibly important.

 HOOKED Students

> I feel like as a senior it was nice to have a class that I felt like I was learning real life skills while also being relaxed.
> ~Carine B.

 ## UNLOCKING the Lesson: Resume

Students create a ready-to-use resume which can be updated and used for years to come.

 ## The NUTS and BOLTS

- Resume Evaluation Worksheet
- Resume Template Worksheet

 ## My CHAIN of Events

1. *Resume Evaluation Worksheet:* Go over the types of resumes with your students (Chronological, Functional, Combination, Targeted). Discuss the differences in the resumes and how different situations and people's work experiences determine which type of resume someone should write. Have the students complete the Resume Evaluation Worksheet. They will be given situations and determine what type of resume should be written in each situation.
2. *Resume Brainstorm Template*: Students will determine what they want to highlight on their own resume and determine which type of resume they will write. They can use the template to brainstorm but will need to create a final typed version.

 ## The GEARS Are Moving

Answer keys are provided for the Resume Evaluation Worksheets. Use the resume section of the digital career portfolio rubric to evaluate students' final resumes.

Digital Career Portfolio Unit ◆ 179

 **KEY Hints**

- **Have students use templates.** No need to reinvent the wheel. There are many programs out there that have resume templates for students to use. Have them find what they like and run with it.

Cover Letter

Most students don't really know what it takes to apply for a career. Some students may have jobs, but they probably had to fill out a short online application to get that job. They probably didn't have to turn in a resume and almost certainly didn't have to turn in a cover letter. Over the years, I have had more and more students who have never even heard of a cover letter. With the advancing of technology, the cover letter may have morphed into the "cover email," the concepts and purpose of the device has not changed.

Having students create a generic cover letter can be a useful tool for them later in life. This initial letter can be saved and tweaked by students as they begin applying for jobs that require more than an application.

 HOOKED Students

> I didn't realize the cover letter is like introducing yourself.
> ~ Bowe S.

 **UNLOCKING the Lesson: Cover Letter**

Students develop a generic cover letter that can be easily tweaked when needed to apply for a job and serve as an important piece of their digital career portfolio.

The NUTS and BOLTS

- Cover Letter Evaluation Worksheet
- Cover Letter Template

 **My CHAIN of Events**

1. *Cover Letter Evaluation Worksheet:* Walk through the "Cover Letter Evaluation" worksheet with your students. Here you will break down the cover letter into different sections and look at examples of how to and how not to create each section.
2. *Cover Letter Template:* Have students use the "Cover Letter Template" to draft their generic cover letter. Explain to students that the cover letter on their digital portfolio will be more generic and not specific to a certain company or position. Students can customize the letter later as needed. They can use the template to brainstorm but will need to create a final typed version.

 The GEARS Are Moving

Answer keys are provided for the Cover Letter Evaluation Worksheets. Use the cover letter section of the digital career portfolio rubric to evaluate students' final cover letters.

 KEY Hints

- **Use a business letter format.** Practice two skills in one by putting the cover letter in a business letter format. Many students have never done this before. Templates can be used as an aid.
- **Practice tweaking the letter to a specific job description.** Show students how they can easily tweak their generic cover letter to a specific job description when needed.

Letters of Recommendation

Over a decade of teaching experience has taught me many things. One of which is that students truly do not know how to ask for a letter of recommendation. I have received many recommendations where the student needs the letter the next day, or they don't tell me what the recommendation is for, or they don't provide a list of their activities and achievements to aid with the writing of the letter. Talk to any teacher and they will tell you the same thing: students don't know how to ask for a letter of recommendation.

Teaching students the proper way to ask for a letter of recommendation accomplishes two things at once. Students will not only learn the etiquette for asking for a letter of recommendation, but they will also receive the letters to use in their portfolio, aiding in their job or college search in the future.

 HOOKED Students

> I never knew there was a proper way to ask for a letter of recommendation!
>
> ~ Evan V.

 **UNLOCKING the Lesson: Letters of Recommendation**

Help students build their digital portfolio with character references, while teaching them the proper way to request a letter of recommendation.

 The NUTS and BOLTS

- Letter of Recommendation Request Etiquette Poster
- Letter of Recommendation Request Form

My CHAIN of Events

1. *Letter of Recommendation Request Etiquette:* Go over the "Etiquette for Requesting a Letter of Recommendation" document with your students.
2. *Letter of Recommendation Request Form:* Have students complete the "Letter of Recommendation Request Form" and ask at least three people (they are not related to) for a letter of recommendation. These letters can be digital, or they can scan a physical letter to a student's digital portfolio.

 The GEARS Are Moving

Assess students on their ability to follow the etiquette protocol when asking for their letters.

 **KEY Hints**

- **Print the 'Etiquette' document as a poster.** Display the poster in your classroom to remind students of the proper way to ask for a letter of recommendation.
- **Have students request letters from contacts other than teachers.** Limit students to getting requests only from teachers. If all students request all their letters from teachers, your colleges will be inundated with requests and probably not be too happy with you (learned this one from experience). Plus, let students know that having requests from a variety of people will only be beneficial to them.

Community Service Project

I have always been passionate about finding a way to give back to others. In high school, I started an event that, over the course of several years, raised tens of thousands of dollars for the American Cancer Society. Not only was I able to give back to a cause in which I felt passionate, I learned several awesome skills about event planning, marketing, and bookkeeping that served me well in my radio career. As the promotions manager of that radio station, I was in charge of many events like the one I organized as a teenager. Those skills I acquired were 100% transferable to the workforce.

It is one thing to lecture and give hypothetical situations about skills needed in the workforce, it's another to put them into a real-life situation. Creating the scenario where students have to learn as they go for a project they are passionate about will not only introduce these skills but will make sure they are a part of their permanent set of skills.

Over the years, students have gone many different directions with the community service project. My work-based learning students have used this project in order to add more volunteer experience to their digital career portfolios. Some groups have collected items for the local animal shelter and other groups collected items for our school-wide food pantry. My marketing students have implemented this project by creating a YouTube show and selling advertising and showing sponsorships and product placements within their show. Students then donated all the proceeds to a local animal rescue. In every situation, students have a memorable experience because they are working on something real and worthwhile all while producing work that someone outside of the school will be witnessing.

 HOOKED Students

It was a fun way to be creative and help others!
~ Alexis W.

 **UNLOCKING the Lesson: Community Service Project**

Develop real-world skills within your students while doing good within the community. Students take pride in their project because they see first-hand the results their efforts produce.

The NUTS and BOLTS

- Community Service Project Materials
- Community Partners

 **My CHAIN of Events**

1. Introduce the project by having students research local charities with the "Community Service Project Research" worksheet. Students will research at least two local charities and find one they would like to partner with to complete their project.
2. Have students create goals for their project with the "Project Goals" worksheet. Students will create SMART goals for their project.
3. Students will then need to plan the project and assign specific roles for each group member.
4. Students complete their respective projects.

 The GEARS Are Moving

After students complete their Community Service Projects, they will create a slideshow reflection and present it to the class. Students will reflect on their success and determine what could have been better. Use the "Project Reflection" assignment and rubric in the project materials.

 **KEY Hints**

- **Contact the local organizations.** Have representatives from the local charities come in and work with the students on their projects. They can help give perspective on what their organization's needs are.
- **Write press releases!** Share the great work of your students with the local news. Show the community the good work your students are doing.

Personal Narrative

Name _____ Period_____ Date _____

What Do You Value? Activity

According to your values sort the "Value Cards" top being the most valued and bottom being least valued.

1. What or who in your life has influenced your values?
_____
_____
_____

2. How do your values influence your daily choices?
_____
_____
_____

Sort the "Value Cards" again based on the following situation: "You are 35 years old wanting to build a new house in the country for you, your spouse, and two kids."

3. Did your values move or stay in the same position? Explain.
_____
_____
_____

Sort the "Value Cards" again based on the following situation: "You just won the lottery and now have $125 million dollars."

4. Did your values move or stay in the same position? Explain.
_____
_____
_____

5. How can changes in your life affect your values?
_____
_____
_____

6. What role do your personal values play when choosing a future career?
_____
_____
_____

Copyright material from Ashley Johnson, *Unlocking the Career and Technical Education Classroom*, 2025, Routledge

What Do You Value? Activity Cards

Education	Health	Freedom
Family	Success	Wealth
Adventure	Community	Faith
Friendship	Happiness	Security
Service	Respect	Appearance
Growth	Fun	Love

Copyright material from Ashley Johnson, *Unlocking the Career and Technical Education Classroom*, 2025, Routledge

Personal Narrative Template

Use the following template to help gather ideas for your personal narrative. Once you have your ideas together, you will need to construct your (at least three paragraphs) personal narrative and include a professional looking photo of yourself. The narrative and the photo will be part of your digital portfolio.

Introduction

This paragraph will introduce the reader to your reasoning for the career path you have chosen. Include a personal story that led you to this career choice.

Body

This/these paragraph(s) will introduce the skills and qualities you possess making you a great fit for this career choice. You can include specific training, classes, or experiences that relate to the field.

Conclusion

This paragraph will summarize the story, passion, and skills you expressed in the intro and body. Restate your reasoning for choosing this career path.

Copyright material from Ashley Johnson, *Unlocking the Career and Technical Education Classroom*, 2025, Routledge

Resume

Name _____ Period_____ __Date _____

Resumé Evaluation Worksheet

Review the different resumé format types below. On the next page, identify which format type should be used in each situation.

Chronological Resumé
The Chronological Resumé is for the person with a lot of work experience and little to no gaps in their work history. The writer will start with their current work position and work backwards, including education at the bottom of the page. In order to keep the resume to one page, the writer will let the work experience speak for itself and not need to include other skills, interests, or miscellaneous information on the resumé. Those items can be highlighted elsewhere in the digital portfolio.

Functional Resumé
The Functional Resumé is for the person who is just graduating high school or college or maybe changing careers. The writer may not have a lot of experience in the related field to which they are applying. The writer will highlight skills, education, training, or awards that would be a good fit for the job for which they are applying. Any type of work experience the writer has will come last on the resumé.

Combination Resumé
The Combination Resumé is for the person who wants to focus on both their work experience and their skills. This resumé is best for someone who has stayed in the same job for many years and also wants to highlight the skills they have acquired over the years. The writer can put the resumé in any order, but has a main focus on work experience and skills/achievements related to the job in which they are applying.

Targeted Resumé
The Targeted Resumé can be in the style of Chronological, Functional, or Combination but is built to focus on the one job to which the writer is applying. The writer will use specific language from the job posting and only put applicable information on the resumé for the job to which they are applying. The writer looks to make their resume look like the perfect applicant for the job posting. An objective statement can be present that mentions the position for which the writer is applying.

Name _____ Period_____ __Date _____

Resumé Evaluation Worksheet

Read each situation and determine which style of resumé would be best for the situation. Then, brainstorm what you want to include on your resume and what style of resumé would be best for you.

Jonathan is a recent college graduate. He doesn't have a lot of work experience, but did hold a part-time job at an ice cream shop while he attended college. Jonathan was involved in many activities in high school and college and was even the student body president.

What type of resumé should Jonathan create? _____

Mary is applying for a specific position in the Marketing department of a company. She would like her resume to highlight the specific skills and requirements that were given in the job posting.

What type of resumé should Mary create? _____

Bill has been working in the plumbing industry for over 25 years. He has no gaps in employment and would like to highlight his extensive work history.

What type of resumé should Bill create? _____

Samantha has been working in the accounting field for 10 years. She has acquired a lot of skills and certifications over the years. She would like to highlight both her work history and her skills and certifications.

What type of resumé should Samantha create? _____

Name _____ Period_____ Date _____

ANSWERS

Resumé Evaluation Worksheet

Read each situation and determine which style of resumé would be best for the situation. Then, brainstorm what you want to include on your resume and what style of resumé would be best for you.

Jonathan is a recent college graduate. He doesn't have a lot of work experience, but did hold a part-time job at an ice cream shop while he attended college. Jonathan was involved in many activities in high school and college and was even the student body president.

What type of resumé should Jonathan create? _____Functional_____

Mary is applying for a specific position in the Marketing department of a company. She would like her resume to highlight the specific skills and requirements that were given in the job posting.

What type of resumé should Mary create? _____Targeted_____

Bill has been working in the plumbing industry for over 25 years. He has no gaps in employment and would like to highlight his extensive work history.

What type of resumé should Bill create? _____Chronological_____

Samantha has been working in the accounting field for 10 years. She has acquired a lot of skills and certifications over the years. She would like to highlight both her work history and her skills and certifications.

What type of resumé should Samantha create? _____Combination_____

Name _____ Period_____ Date _____

Resumé Brainstorm Template

Use the following brainstorming boxes to determine what you can highlight in each section of your resumé.

Education

Work History

Skills/Certifications/Awards

Personality Test Results

What type of resume is best for you?_____

Copyright material from Ashley Johnson, *Unlocking the Career and Technical Education Classroom*, 2025, Routledge

Cover Letter

Name _____ Period _____ Date _____

Cover Letter Evaluation Worksheet

Below is an example of a well constructed cover letter. You will break down each part of the cover letter and go over ways to create each section.

Ashley Johnson
123 Main Street   **Header**
City, IN 45678

To Whom It May Concern: **Salutation**

Intro Paragraph

I am writing with the objective of obtaining a job in the teaching profession. Since the age of 12, I have always been interested in teaching and working with those younger than me. I remember forcing my younger sister and cousins to be my "students" and giving them homework assignments over our summer breaks. Ever since, I have made it my mission to grow as an educator to be the best I can in the classroom.

Body Paragraph

I just graduated with my degree in Elementary Education and finished my student teaching at Best School. I learned valuable techniques and tricks of the trade from my mentor teacher, Mrs. Smith. I have created an extensive vocabulary unit for 2nd grade students that will give me a leg up as I transition to my own classroom. I am a very outgoing person and love working with other people. I would love to team up with other classrooms and collaborate on projects with teachers throughout the school. I have a system set up for consistent communication with parents, so we can give our kids the best chance for success.

Closing Paragraph

Again, I am very excited to find a position to kickstart my teaching career. I am a great team player and feel I would be an asset to your school. I would love to talk more and schedule an interview. Please contact me by phone (260) 222-3333 or email (emailaddress@gmail.com). Thank you for your time!

Sincerely,   **Letter Ending**

Ashley Johnson   **Signature**

Copyright material from Ashley Johnson, *Unlocking the Career and Technical Education Classroom*, 2025, Routledge

Name _____ Period_____ __Date _____

Cover Letter Evaluation Worksheet

Review the different sections of the cover letter and decide which examples are professional.

Header

Your header consists of your name and address in proper mailing address format. Circle the Header you feel is professional and in proper format.

Rebekah Smith	132 Main Street	Rebekah Smith	Rebekah Smith
132 main street	Butler, IN 47888	132 Main Street	132 Main Street Butler IN 47888
butler in 47888	Rebekah Smith	Butler, IN 47888	

Salutation

Your salutation is your greeting to the reader. If you know who the letter is going to, you should address that person specifically. If you do not know who the letter is going to, a more generic greeting can be used. Circle the salutations that you feel are professional and proper (there is more than one right answer).

Dear Mr. Baker,   Hey,   To Whom It May Concern,   What's Up,   Dear Hiring Manager,

Intro Paragraph

Your introductory paragraph will include the type of job/career that interests you. You will also describe how you came to your career decision. You may want to use a specific story or example. Circle the paragraph you feel is the best introductory paragraph.

I am writing because I would like to get a job. I am in need of extra money because my car needs a new transmission. Any job you have would be great.

I am writing to express my interest in a job in the medical field. I have always has a fascination with the human body and how it works. As a kid, I even did multiple science fair projects how different parts of the body worked. My favorite project was my "Hip Hop Heart" project on irregular heartbeats. I am excited to continue to grow my knowledge as I begin my healthcare career.

I am writing because I am interestested in obtaining a job in the field of finance. I have multiple financial certifications and just graduated with my associate's degree in accounting.

Name _____ Period _____ Date _____

Cover Letter Evaluation Worksheet

Review the different sections of the cover letter and decide which examples are professional.

Body Paragraph

Your body paragraph will describe the skills, training, and qualities you have that make you a good fit for the career choice and a team player. Circle the following items that would be appropriate for someone looking for a job in the business field to include in their body paragraph (more than one right answer).

Top 5 Clifton Strengths	Summer Internship at a Local Accounting Firm	Favorite TV Show
High School Baseball Batting Average	Collaboration Skills	The 4H Awards you received in High School
Google Certification	Microsoft Programs Used	Current Electronic Filing System You Created
AP Biology Grade	Examples of Leadership Roles	Story of Childhood Pet

Closing Paragraph

Your closing paragraph will summarize the first two paragraphs and ask for an interview. You will give your contact information (phone number and email) so the reader can get in touch with you. Circle the paragraph that you feel is the best closing paragraph.

Thanks for your time. Give me a call if you want to get together and chat (230-555-8888). You can also email me at emailaddress@gmail.com.

I am so excited to utilize my training and skills into a career I am so passionate about. I would love to sit down and speak with you more. Please feel free to email (emailaddress@gmail.com) or call me (260-555-8888) to set up a time for an interview. Thank you for your time!

Letter Ending

Your letter ending should be a professional end to your cover letter. Circle the proper/professional letter endings. (More than one right answer)

Sincerely,   Later Gator,   Peace Out,   Best Regards,   Respectfully,

Signature

For a digital portfolio, use a font that looks like a signature but is still legible.

Name _____ Period_____ Date _____

Cover Letter Evaluation Worksheet

Review the different sections of the cover letter and decide which examples are professional.

Header

Your header consists of your name and address in proper mailing address format. Circle the Header you feel is professional and in proper format.

Rebekah Smith
132 main street
butler in 47888

132 Main Street
Butler, IN 47888
Rebekah Smith

> Rebekah Smith
> 132 Main Street
> Butler, IN 47888

Rebekah Smith
132 Main Street Butler IN 47888

Salutation

Your salutation is your greeting to the reader. If you know who the letter is going to, you should address that person specifically. If you do not know who the letter is going to, a more generic greeting can be used. Circle the salutations that you feel are professional and proper (there is more than one right answer).

>Dear Mr. Baker,   Hey,   >To Whom It May Concern,   What's Up,   >Dear Hiring Manager,

Intro Paragraph

Your introductory paragraph will include the type of job/career that interests you. You will also describe how you came to your career decision. You may want to use a specific story or example. Circle the paragraph you feel is the best introductory paragraph.

I am writing because I would like to get a job. I am in need of extra money because my car needs a new transmission. Any job you have would be great.

> I am writing to express my interest in a job in the medical field. I have always has a fascination with the human body and how it works. As a kid, I even did multiple science fair projects how different parts of the body worked. My favorite project was my "Hip Hop Heart" project on irregular heartbeats. I am excited to continue to grow my knowledge as I begin my healthcare career.

I am writing because I am interestested in obtaining a job in the field of finance. I have multiple financial certifications and just graduated with my associate's degree in accounting.

Name _____ Period _____ Date _____

Cover Letter Evaluation Worksheet

Review the different sections of the cover letter and decide which examples are professional.

Body Paragraph

Your body paragraph will describe the skills, training, and qualities you have that make you a good fit for the career choice and a team player. Circle the following items that would be appropriate for someone looking for a job in the business field to include in their body paragraph (more than one right answer).

- **Top 5 Clifton Strengths**
- **Summer Internship at a Local Accounting Firm**
- Favorite TV Show
- High School Baseball Batting Average
- **Collaboration Skills**
- The 4H Awards you received in High School
- **Google Certification**
- **Microsoft Programs Used**
- **Current Electronic Filing System You Created**
- AP Biology Grade
- **Examples of Leadership Roles**
- Story of Childhood Pet

Closing Paragraph

Your closing paragraph will summarize the first two paragraphs and ask for an interview. You will give your contact information (phone number and email) so the reader can get in touch with you. Circle the paragraph that you feel is the best closing paragraph.

Thanks for your time. Give me a call if you want to get together and chat (230-555-8888). You can also email me at emailaddress@gmail.com.

I am so excited to utilize my training and skills into a career I am so passionate about. I would love to sit down and speak with you more. Please feel free to email (emailaddress@gmail.com) or call me (260-555-8888) to set up a time for an interview. Thank you for your time!

Letter Ending

Your letter ending should be a professional end to your cover letter. Circle the proper/professional letter endings. (More than one right answer)

- **Sincerely,**
- Later Gator,
- Peace Out,
- **Best Regards,**
- **Respectfully,**

Signature

For a digital portfolio, use a font that looks like a signature but is still legible.

Name _____ Period_____ Date _____

Cover Letter Template

Header
Your Name _____
Your Street Address _____
Your City, State Zip _____

Salutation
To Whom It May Concern,

Introduction Paragraph
Here you will describe the type job/career that interests you. Describe why you came to this career decision.

Body Paragraph
Here you will describe the skills, training, and qualities you have that make you a good team player and fit for this career path.

Closing Paragraph
Here you will summarize the first two paragraphs and give your contact information (phone number/email) so someone can get ahold of you.

Letter Ending
Sincerely,

Signature

Letters of Recommendation

Copyright material from Ashley Johnson, *Unlocking the Career and Technical Education Classroom*, 2025, Routledge

Etiquette for Requesting a Letter of Recommendation

Ask The Right Person

When asking someone for a letter of recommendation, you should not ask just anyone. The person should be someone you have known for at least a year, be able to give positive examples of your work ethic and skills, and NOT be related to you.

Give Ample Time with a Clear Deadline

Give the writer time to write the letter. Do NOT ask someone to write a letter of recommendation you need the next day. Give the writer at least two weeks to write the letter and provide an exact date in which you need it.

Provide Details

Tell the writer the purpose of the letter. Give them a list of accomplishments, work history, awards, and activities to make their writing process go more smoothly.

Follow Up with a Thank You

Send a hand written thank you note to the writer. They took time to help you, so take time to thank them!

Letter of Recommendation Request

Thank you for writing a letter of recommendation for me. Please find information below that will hopefully make the writing process easier for you.

Name: _____ **Nickname:** _____

Purpose of Letter: General   Scholarship   Job   College Admission   Other: _____

Letter Deadline: _____ **Format of Letter:** Digital   Hard Copy

Address Letter To: _____

Deliver Letter To: _____

Extracurricular Activities (in/out of school) Include number of participated years.
_____
_____
_____
_____
_____
_____

Work/Volunteer Experience (in/out of school) Include number of participated years.
_____
_____
_____
_____
_____

Awards
_____
_____
_____
_____

Copyright material from Ashley Johnson, *Unlocking the Career and Technical Education Classroom*, 2025, Routledge

Honors/AP/Dual Credit Courses
_____
_____
_____

Certifications
_____
_____
_____

Hobbies/Interests
_____
_____
_____

Grade Point Average _____ **Diploma Type** _____

Education/ Career Goals
_____
_____
_____
_____

Other Important Information
_____
_____
_____
_____
_____
_____
_____
_____
_____

Community Service Project

Name _____ Period_____ Date _____

Community Service Project Research ♡

You will be participating in a community service project. Your group will research two local charities. Record your research below. You will be presenting this information to the class.

Organization Name: _____

Organization Address: _____

Organization Phone Number: _____

What does this organization do?

_____
_____
_____
_____

How could we, as a class, help this organization?

_____
_____
_____

Organization Name: _____

Organization Address: _____

Organization Phone Number: _____

What does this organization do?

_____
_____
_____
_____

How could we, as a class, help this organization?

_____
_____
_____

Name _____ Period_____ __Date _____

Project Goals

Create SMART goals to help you measure the traction and success of your project.

S
Specific - In detail, describe what you are looking to achieve.

M
Measurable - How will you measure your success? (money raised, items collected, people served, etc.)

A
Achievable - Is this goal something that can be achieved with the resources and time available?

R
Relevant - Does this goal help solve a problem specific to the organization you are trying to help?

T
Timeline - When does your goal need to be complete?

Copyright material from Ashley Johnson, *Unlocking the Career and Technical Education Classroom*, 2025, Routledge

Name _____ Period _____ Date _____

Planning the Project ♡

After voting on one community service project use this sheet to plan the project as a class. Elect a project Manager to organize and record the plan.

Name of Organization: _____
Organization Contact Information: _____
Date of Project: _____
Describe the Project:
_____
_____
_____
_____

Name	Role

Copyright material from Ashley Johnson, Unlocking the Career and Technical Education Classroom, 2025, Routledge

Name _____ Period _____ __Date _____

Project Reflection ♡

After completing the community service project, your group will put together a slideshow reflecting on your success and present it to the class. Your presentation needs to include the following elements:

- Overview of the organization the project was helping
- Goals of the project
- Roles and responsibilities of the members of your team
- Project progression
- Final project results
- Reflection (Did you meet your goals? What would you do differently if you did the project again?)

	Novice	Limited	Developing	Mastery
Mechanics	Slideshow has less than four slides, has no structure and is hard to follow, and contains many spelling/grammar errors.	Slideshow has four or five slides, is hard to follow, and contains several spelling/grammar errors.	Slideshow has five or six slides, is easy to follow, and contains minimal spelling/grammar errors.	Slideshow has a minimum of seven slides, is visually appealing, and contains little to no spelling/grammar errors.
Organization Overview	Overview of the organization is confusion with no mission. None of the following deatils are given: what they do, who they help, and how they help.	Minimal overview of the organization is given with a slight mission. Details include at least one of the following: what they do, who they help, and how they help.	An overview of the organization is given with an overall mission. Details include most of the following: what they do, who they help, and how they help.	A detailed overview of the organization is given with an overall mission. Details include all of the following: what they do, who they help, and how they help.
Project Goals	Project goals are confusing and do not follow the SMART Goal format.	Minimal overview of the project goals are given and slightly follow the SMART Goal format.	An overview of the project goals are given and mostly follow the SMART Goal format.	A detailed overview of the project goals are given and follow the SMART Goal format.
Roles and Responsibilities	Roles and responsibilities are unclear for the team.	Roles and responsibilities are given but unclear which team member is responsible for what.	An overview of the roles and responsibilities for each member of the team is given.	A detailed overview of the roles and responsibilities for each member of the team is clear and given.
Project Progression	A timeline of the progress of the project is not given showing no steps taken to complete the project.	A vague timeline of the progress of the project is given showing few steps taken to complete the project.	A timeline of the progress of the project is given showing the steps taken to complete the project.	A detailed timeline of the progress of the project is given showing detailed steps taken to complete the project.
Final results	The results of the project are unclear.	A vague report of the project is given with few numbers showing results of the project.	A final report of the project is given including numbers showing results of the project.	A detailed final report of the project is given including numbers showing the detailed results of the project.
Reflection	Reflection is minimal and confusing and does not include the following: proud moments, if goals were met, what could be improved upon.	A vauge reflection is given on the results of the project including at least one of the following: proud moments, if goals were met, what could be improved upon.	A reflection is given on the results of the project including most of the following: proud moments, if goals were met, what could be improved upon.	A detailed reflection is given on the results of the project including all of the following: proud moments, if goals were met, what could be improved upon.

Copyright material from Ashley Johnson, *Unlocking the Career and Technical Education Classroom*, 2025, Routledge

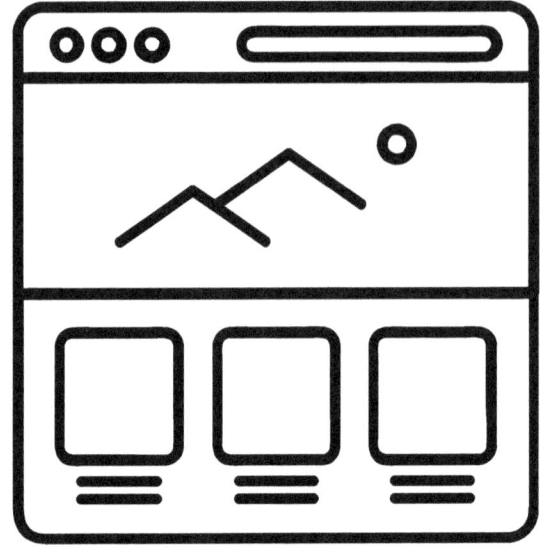

Digital Career Portfolio Materials and Rubric

Copyright material from Ashley Johnson, Unlocking the Career and Technical Education Classroom, 2025, Routledge

Digital Portfolio Checklist

Portfolio URL

_____

- [ ] Personal Narrative
- [ ] Photo
- [ ] Resume
- [ ] Cover Letter
- [ ] Letters of Recommendation (Three)
- [ ] Extracurricular/ Community Service Activities
- [ ] Certifications and Awards
- [ ] Other Examples of Work and Skills

Name _____ Period_____ Date _____

Certifications, Awards, and Other Examples of Work & Skills

Use this worksheet to help plan the certifications, awards and other examples of Work and Skills sections of your portfolio. After you have your thoughts on paper, create a visually appealing digital version to be included in your **Final Digital Portfolio.**

Certifications:

Certification:	Date Issued:
Certification:	Date Issued:

Awards

Award:	Date Awarded:
Award:	Date Awarded:
Award:	Date Awarded:
Award:	Date Awarded:

In School Activities:

Athletics:	Arts:
Clubs:	Other:

Name _____ Period_____ __Date _____

Outside of School Activities:

Athletics:	Arts:

Clubs:	Other:

Community Service/Volunteer Activities:

Activity:	Hours:

Description:

Activity:	Hours:

Description:

Activity:	Hours:

Description:

Name _____ Period_____ __Date _____

Examples of Work:

Examples of projects, tasks, or events that show your work ethic:

Skills:

Skills you have that would like to highlight:

Personality Test Results:

Results of professional personality tests (i.e. Myers-Briggs, Clifton Strengths)

Other:

Digital Career Portfolio Rubric

	Novice	Limited	Developing	Mastery
Personal Narrative	Narrative does not include any personal stories or examples. No picture is included.	A written summary of the student's life experiences that lead to their particular school/career choices is included. Narrative includes few stories and examples, but doesn't really give an insight to the student personally. Picture is included but not professional.	A written summary of the student's life experiences that lead to their particular school/career choices is included. Narrative includes stories and examples that give a glimpse into the student's personal life. A professional headshot of the student is included.	A written summary of the student's life experiences that lead to their particular school/career choices is included. Narrative includes personal stories and examples that allow the reader to get to know the student on a deeper level than a resume would. A professional headshot of the student is included.
Resume	Resume is not present or does not summarize the portfolio and cannot stand alone.	Resume somewhat summarizes the digital portfolio, but doesn't really encourage the reader to continue exploring the portfolio. The resume has a difficult time standing alone.	Resume acts as a one-page summary of the entire digital portfolio. The resume can stand on its own if the reader is in a time crunch or asks for the single document.	Resume acts as a one-page summary of the entire digital portfolio, that entices the reader to continue to review the entire portfolio. The resume can stand on its own if the reader is in a time crunch or asks for the single document.
Cover Letter	Cover letter is not present or is unclear in its purpose. No mention of student goals, skills, or qualities.	Cover letter is present but does not address goals for the future or what the student is looking for in a college or employment. Student does not mention skills and qualities that would make them a valuable member of the team.	Cover letter addresses goals for the immediate future and highlights what the student is looking for in a college or place of employment. Student vaguely touch on skills and qualities that would make them a valuable member of the team.	Cover letter pinpoints goals for the immediate future and lays out what the student is looking for in a college or place of employment. Student highlights skills and qualities that would make them a valuable member of the team.
Letters of Recommendation	No letters are present or they do not include skills and qualities of the student. Letter does not read favorably for the student.	At least one letter of recommendation is present which includes skills and qualities that read favorably for the student.	More than one letter of recommendation is present which include skills and qualities that would make the student an asset to a team. Letters focus is geared towards the goals of the student.	Multiple letters of recommendation are present, highlighting the skills and qualities that would make the student an asset to a team. Letters focus on specific area of study or career field of the student.
Extracurricular/ Community Service Activities	Little to no overview of the student's extracurricular/ community service activities.	A vague overview is given of the extracurricular/ community service (in and out of school) activities in which the student has participated.	A specific overview is given of the extracurricular/ community service (in and out of school) activities in which the student has participated.	A visually appealing and specific representation of the extracurricular/ community service (in and out of school) activities in which the student has participated is included.
Certifications and Awards	Little to no overview of the certifications/awards a student has received.	A vague overview is given of the certifications/awards (in and out of school) a student has received.	A specific overview is given of the certifications/awards (in and out of school) the student has received.	A visually appealing representation of the certifications/awards (in and out of school) a student has received is included.
Other Examples of Work and Technical Skills	Little to no overview of other work and technical skills that students can show to support their qualification for entrance to the school/ employment.	A vague overview is given of other work and technical skills that students can show to support their qualification for entrance to the school/ employment.	A specific overview is given of other work and technical skills that students can show to support their qualification for entrance to the school/ employment.	A visually appealing representation of other work and technical skills that students can show to support their qualification for entrance to the school/ employment is included.
Website Appearance and Flow	Digital portfolio is not visually appealing and difficult to navigate. Portfolio does not make the student look favorable to colleges or employers, and would frustrate the user to try and navigate.	Digital portfolio contains good information but navigation does not flow well. Portfolio would frustrate the user to try and navigate.	Digital portfolio is clear and contains all the information needed to make the student stand out from the competition.	Digital portfolio is visually appealing and easy to navigate. Portfolio makes the student stand out from other candidates.

6

Content Consumption Unit

Delivering content in a way other than lecture can sometimes be hard to incorporate. Students need a variety of delivery methods to stay engaged and consume the material presented. It can be exhausting trying to come up with multiple ways to engage students in your course work, especially when teaching multiple classes throughout the day.

In this unit, you will find activities to help students with vocabulary in the "Word Wall" lesson, interactive ways to incorporate book studies and current industry articles, and a gamification element which can be used for projects. Intertwining these activities with the curriculum you already have in place will give you the mix up you need to keep kids engaged while incorporating student choice.

Word Walls

When I was in high school, I had to complete the same vocabulary assignment in almost every class: get out a piece of loose-leaf paper, write and underline the vocabulary word, and use the textbook to write the definition word-for-word. Do you remember doing this? Did you have any educational epiphanies due to this activity? No. Me either. In fact, the only thing I do remember from these vocabulary assignments was the ink stain left on my hand after writing 20 terms and definitions (if you're left-handed you understand what I'm talking about).

The only class where discussing vocabulary words wasn't completed in this fashion was in business class with Mrs. Surfus. She has a vocabulary activity classifying terms into categories and defending why we put them into that category. I remember this activity, and many business terms, over 20 years later because I had ownership in the activity and my learning.

"Word Walls" aren't new; teachers have been using them for years. HOW I use "Word Walls" and activities to incorporate those key terms is what makes all the difference. By giving students the wheel to drive which words end up on the wall and creating assignments that include student voice instead of a regurgitated definition, students actually learn and retain the information.

 HOOKED Students

I like finding terms as I read rather than being given words to look for.

~ Jake A.

Word Walls give me control of my own learning.

~ Evan W.

The flip chart activity gave me a chance to color, which is fun.

~ Allyson K.

 **UNLOCKING the Lesson: Word Wall**

Students take charge of their learning by identifying key terms from books, articles, or videos as they arise in class. Integrating these terms into classroom activities and assignments empowers student engagement while increasing comprehension and retention.

 **The NUTS and BOLTS**

- Sticky notes/index cards
- Highlighters
- Wall/board space
- Key Term activities

 My CHAIN of Events

1. Create specific wall/board space for the "Word Wall."
2. As students read articles and books, watch videos, or participate in class discussion, have them highlight or write terms on sticky notes or index cards. Terms can be words students don't know, need clarified, or find important.
3. Sort through student term submissions, and place recurring words on the "Word Wall." Discuss the meaning and importance of each of these terms.
4. Throughout the unit or project, assign "Word Wall" activities/assignments to reinforce student learning.

"Word Wall" Flip Chart Activity

1. Print the "Word Wall" Flip Chart Activity (one copy of the set allows for students to create flip charts for four terms. If you want students to create more than four flip charts, make multiple copies of the sets for each student).
2. Students choose terms from the "Word Wall" they wish to create for flip charts.
3. On the "term" flap, students write the term and draw a picture representing the term.
4. On the "definition" flap, students define the word in their own words.
5. On the "How will understanding this term benefit you?" flap, students describe how understanding this term will benefit them in the future.
6. Students cut out the "term" flap and the "definition" flap.

7. Students stack "term" flap on top of the "definition" flap and then on top of the "How will understanding this term benefit you?" box on the second sheet.
8. Students secure the flaps with glue or a staple and turn in the Flip Chart worksheet (see example in "Word Wall" Flip Chart Activity materials).

Term Table Jams

1. Print the "Term Table Jams" worksheet for each student.
2. Instruct students to write a song or poem using at least five terms from the "Word Wall."
3. Students will write their song/poem around the record on the "Term Table."

Student Made Matching Game

1. Print the "Word Wall Match Game" pages front-to-back.
2. Put students into groups of four to five students.
3. Students will use two cards per "Word Wall" word. On one card they will write the term, and on the other card, they will draw a picture representing the term.
4. Once the game is complete, students will lay the cards face down on the table. They will take turns turning over two cards. If they get a match, they keep the match. The student with the most matches at the end of the game is the winner.

 The GEARS Are Moving

Three choices are given for a final assessment: creating a "Word Wall" Whisper, producing a podcast episode, or writing a blog post. Assessment details and rubric are provided in the materials.

 **KEY Hints**

- **Create a new "Word Wall" for each unit.** For each unit or project, create a new "Word Wall." "Word Walls" can stay

up all year but label each "Word Wall" by unit or project to act as a reminder of terms and the related course work associated with terms.
- **Make "Word Wall" submissions anonymous.** Sometimes students don't ask for clarification because they fear looking "dumb" to their peers. By having students submit anonymously with the instruction to submit words that meet one of three criteria (I don't know this word, I need clarification on this word, and I think this word is important) students are more likely to participate without fear of scrutiny.
- **Give students a choice when it comes to activities.** You don't always have to use the same activities or assignments when assessing the students' understanding of the terms. Mix it up, or better yet give the students a choice which activity they want to do.
- **Host a Poetry Slam**. Set up your room like a coffee house. Serve refreshments and have students recite their poems/songs.
- **Print "Word Wall Match Game" cards on cardstock.** To make the cards more durable for play, print them on heavier paper. You may even want to laminate the cards once the students have completed them.

Book Studies

In one of my first years of teaching, I was asking students why they signed up for the class. One student said, "Because I don't want to read." Other students nodded their heads in agreement. I was confused and asked why they thought they wouldn't have to read. "Business is all about numbers," was the response.

My heart hurt because I love to read books on business practices, investing, and marketing. I explained to my students that one of the most common traits among millionaires is that they read, on average, one nonfiction book a month. The only way to stay on top of trends and to continue to grow as a person is to read. This is when I decided to start incorporating book studies in my business classes.

Now, be forewarned, when you tell your students they will be doing a book study, they probably won't hoot and holler with excitement... yet! If you present and execute this in the right way, your students will not only accept reading, they will come back for more.

 HOOKED Students

I liked learning about how successful people manage their money differently, and how there are many different ways to stay out of debt.

~ Will H.

Doing book studies was very engaging and helpful because it gave advice and insight from experienced people in the financial world. I enjoyed that I could go back into the book and look deeper into the information provided to get a better sense of what would benefit me best financially in the future.

~ Lydia Y.

 **UNLOCKING the Lesson: Book Studies**

Students can master standards while staying on top of current industry trends. Reading current trade publications while learning industry jargon and reflecting on real-world application makes books studies academic and relevant.

 **The NUTS and BOLTS**

- Books for each member of the class
- Book study material printables

 My CHAIN of Events

1. First preread the book and make sure it is a good fit for the class.

2. Then, decide how to break up the book. I typically focus on one chapter a day and integrate other lessons into the class period.
3. Fill out due dates on the bookmark page and make copies for each student so they can easily keep track of deadlines while reading.
4. Give students a brief overview of what the book will be about. Read the back cover and possibly some reviews of the book. This will give students an idea of the book's contents and what they want to get from it.
5. Have students complete the "goals" page of their book study materials.
6. Have students fill out a worksheet for each chapter.
7. Once students finish the book, have them reflect on what they have learned. Revisit their initial goals and complete the wrap-up worksheet.

 The GEARS Are Moving

Chapter worksheets can be graded as you work through the book. Three choices are given for a final assessment: creating a book jacket, producing a podcast episode, or writing a book report. Assessment details and rubric are provided in the material printables.

 KEY Hints

- **Explain the difference between fiction and nonfiction.** Nonfiction books lend themselves nicely to business classes. When students can see the relevance these books can have on their career and financial future, their ears perk up.
- **Choose the right book.** Make sure the book is an easy to read and grade appropriate and doesn't have too much technical jargon (although some is needed to add to the students' technical vocabulary). If you, as the teacher,

could sit down and read the book front-to-back in a few hours, then it is perfect for a book study that will last a few weeks in your classroom.
- **Use the Word Wall lesson simultaneously.** The Word Wall lesson works well with book studies when presented with technical jargon used in the book.
- **Print bookmarks on colored cardstock.** This way they will last a little longer than regular paper.
- **Incorporate the reading into class time.** If you assign the student to read at home, you will lose them before you even start. We read the book together in class. This can look a number of ways: reading to the students as they follow along, popcorn reading, or listening to the audio version. Whatever way you choose, make sure you do this in short segments to prevent drifting. I typically don't do more than one chapter at a time. We have 90-minute class periods, so we complete our book study in an allotted period of time and then move to another assignment for the day.
- **Have students keep books in class.** Unless they need to take them home to catch up from missed days, keep books in class. This way there is no excuse not to participate.
- **Invite guest speakers into class.** Industry professionals can bring different perspectives on the topic and can answer real-world questions students may have.
- **Measure levels of engagement with the book.** If students are not engaged, you may want to try a different book next year. If they really enjoyed it, make sure to keep it on your list for future classes.

Badges and Brags

A few years ago, I started teaching an Entrepreneurship class. The goal of this class included students growing their businesses and professional skills. I wanted to encourage students to take risks. However, risk can lead to failure, which is okay. It's an opportunity to learn from those failures.

The way school is structured, students are programmed to think only bad can come from failure. A few years ago, a student asked for extra credit because she was getting an A minus in my class. She explained that her parents would ground her if she had an A minus. This girl was so afraid of "failing" in the eyes of her parents so she was unable to enjoy the process of learning. In an attempt to build a classroom culture that values growth over grades, I created the "Badges and Brags" wall.

The "Badges and Brags" wall is a way for students to work toward goals no matter how many times it takes them to achieve that goal. It also allows students to work at their own pace and move ahead as soon as they are ready. I created *"required"* and *"above and beyond"* badges students could earn as they created and grew their businesses.

As students started earning badges, I noticed there were successes achieved beyond these badges. This is why we added the "brags" section and took time to share our brags with the class. These brags could be anything from making contact with a mentor to hitting a certain number of likes on a social media post.

 HOOKED Students

The 'Badges and Brags Wall' gives students something to work toward rather than a grade.
~ Connor W.

I liked getting to write my accomplishments on the Brags section.
~ Preston B.

 **UNLOCKING the Lesson: Badges and Brags**

This gamification tracking system creates ongoing excitement within a project to encourage growth over grades. Students earn badges and are provided a space to declare self-successes with this "merit badge" system for the classroom.

 **The NUTS and BOLTS**

- Sticky Notes
- "Badges and Brags" Posters & Milestone Badges

 My CHAIN of Events

1. Print "Badges and Brags" posters for each group.
2. Create badges for the milestones of our business project. (Examples: creating a logo, developing a mission statement, creating a pitch deck, etc.)
3. Hang the posters around the room and hang a poster with all the "badges" available to earn.
4. As student groups progress through project milestones, add "badges" to their posters.
5. Students can add "brags" to their posters when they accomplish something they are particularly proud of. (These "brags" could be something like "We set up at the local farmers market" or "We just hit 250 followers on Instagram").
6. Celebrate the "brags" with students!

 The GEARS Are Moving

Assign points to each of the milestone badges. As students earn their badges they can be recorded as grades.

 **KEY Hints**

- **Create "required" milestone badges and "above and beyond" badges.** This will give students who finish early opportunities to continue their growth.
- **Assign due dates for badges.** To keep students moving in a productive manner, assign due dates to badges and milestones.

- **Give the opportunity to revise.** If students don't quite meet the expectations for the milestone badge, give them the opportunity to correct their work and earn the badge, promoting the "growth over grades" model.
- **Celebrate Brags!** Make time for students to announce their "brags" to the class. Not only do they feel good about their accomplishments, but also it helps motivate other students to continue in their work as well.

Article Annotations

More and more schools are moving towards open-source materials instead of classroom textbooks. Or, if they do have textbooks, they are extremely old. Students recognize when textbooks or materials are out of date and lose interest when they feel the materials they are using are irrelevant.

Using article annotations in your classroom is a perfect way to get up-to-date, relevant materials in front of your students, increasing their buy-in to the lesson. And the best part, you can get the most recent trends and information from your industry in front of your students.

Whatever the topic you are covering in your class, you can easily find a relevant article to introduce to your students. Students respond positively to this type of content consumption for a number of reasons: they recognize the information is current and relevant, an article with a few pages is far less intimidating than a textbook, and they see that you as teacher are always looking to increase your knowledge through research.

 HOOKED Students

> Article annotations help me better understand what I'm reading, and asking questions about the text gets me thinking about how to apply it.
>
> ~ Lydia Y.

Article Annotations help me focus on my reading while comprehending it better. I feel more engaged and think through how it is relevant to my life and business.

~ Kyla L.

 **UNLOCKING the Lesson: Article Annotations**

Keep students engaged with current industry publications. Students learn the importance of staying educated throughout life in their current field of study, by reading up-to-date industry findings.

 The NUTS and BOLTS

- Article Annotation Worksheet
- Article Annotation Rubric
- Current Industry Articles
- Highlighters (optional)

 My CHAIN of Events

1. Find a current industry article based on what you are currently talking about in class. For my Entrepreneurship class, I use articles from Forbes.com or even articles shared with my network on LinkedIn.
2. Print the article along with the article annotation worksheet and rubric for each student. I prefer to have students print out the article so they can physically annotate, but if you prefer, you could have them do it all digitally.
3. Have students annotate the article and answer the questions on the article annotation worksheet.
4. Repeat as often as you wish! The best part of this assignment is that it is always different because each article is different. My Entrepreneurships students complete about one article a week.

The GEARS Are Moving

A rubric is included which can be used for each article annotation assigned.

 KEY Hints

- **Complete the first article together as a class.** To get the students familiar with the process, read and complete the first article together. This is especially important if you plan on doing multiple article annotations throughout the year so students know what is expected.
- **Use with "Word Walls."** Have students vote on words from each article to add to a "Word Wall." Students feel a sense of ownership when they pick their own vocabulary words.
- **Have students "grade" each other.** To work on improving our giving and receiving feedback skills, have students use the rubric to grade each other. Then, give students the opportunity to fix or adjust their answers before turning in the assignment.
- **Have different colored highlighters.** I have a bin of different colored highlighters for students to use to do their annotating. I know it sounds silly, but some students get excited about which color they will use and some like to change it up with each article.

Guest Speakers

A few years ago, I had some students in my Entrepreneurship class that were doing really well with their business ideas. We were in the middle of competition season, and I had been giving them some suggestions to expand their businesses. They had been dragging their feet on my suggestions for a couple months. Then, one day I had a guest speaker come in to provide some one-on-one coaching for my student entrepreneurs.

These students had a fabulous one-on-one with the guest who had a few suggestions for them to implement in their business (the same suggestions I had been giving them for months). Of course, they thought these suggestions were brilliant and immediately started implanting them.

Now, it wasn't that they didn't trust my advice. It's just that sometimes when students hear the same voice every day, everything blends together. (Kind of like when you tell your own kids the same thing repeatedly and then someone else tells them that exact thing, they listen the first time.)

Having guest speakers in your classroom helps mix things up and cut through the daily noise. Speakers can give a different perspective, bring their industry expertise, and give student the opportunity to interact with community members.

 HOOKED Students

I like getting to talk with guest speakers because they are out in the real world and can give great advice.
~ Jama G.

The feedback from guest speakers has been so helpful for our business.
~ Saffron W.

 **UNLOCKING the Lesson: Guest Speakers**

Provide your students with the opportunity to interact with industry professionals by inviting guest speakers into your classroom.

 **The NUTS and BOLTS**

- Guest Speaker worksheet

My CHAIN of Events

1. Invite a guest speaker into your classroom.
2. Give students the guest speaker worksheet so they can do some research on the speaker and come up with questions to ask when the speaker is present.
3. Students complete the worksheet while the speaker attends the class. Students will record key takeaways and memorable quotes.

The GEARS Are Moving

Evaluate the students' "Guest Speaker" worksheets to see their takeaways from the speaker.

KEY Hints

- **Use some of the speaker quotes to make a poster.** Make a poster with photos and some of the students' quotes from their worksheet. Display these posters in the classroom so students are reminded of the speaker all year long.

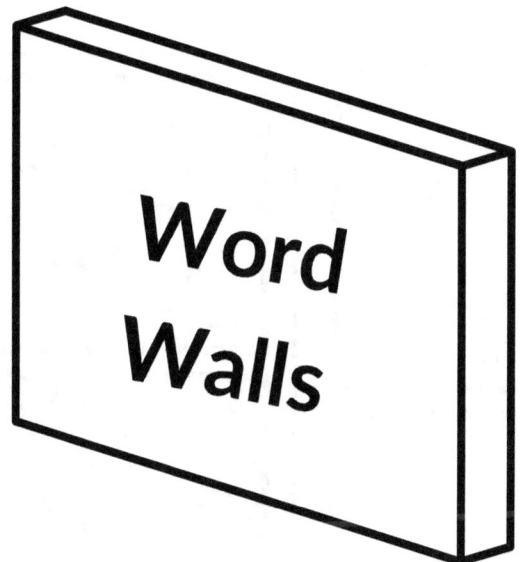

Copyright material from Ashley Johnson, *Unlocking the Career and Technical Education Classroom*, 2025, Routledge

Word Wall Flip Chart Activity

Term

Dog

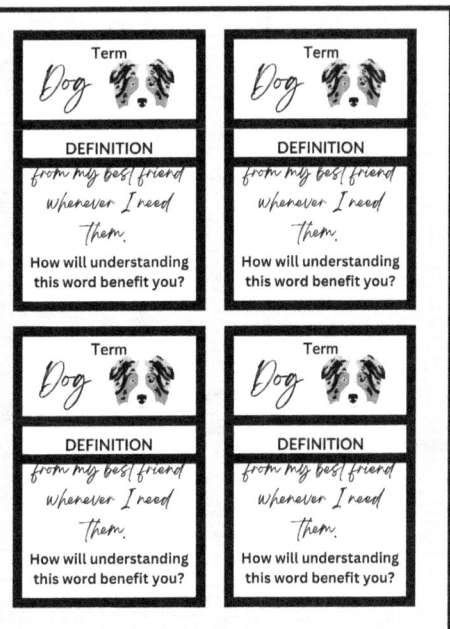

Example

A dog is a pet and loyal best friend to all. Typically has four legs and a tail.

DEFINITION

Knowing I have the opportunity to have a dog as a pet will guarantee cuddles from my best friend whenever I need them.

How will understanding this word benefit you?

Copyright material from Ashley Johnson, Unlocking the Career and Technical Education Classroom, 2025, Routledge

Word Wall Flip Chart Activity

Follow the following steps to complete your Word Wall Flip Chart:
1. On the "Term" flap, write a term from the Word Wall. (one term per flap). Then draw a picture or graphic on the flap that represents the term.
2. On the "Definition" flap, define the term in your own words.
3. On the "How . . . " flap, describe how understanding this term will benefit you.
4. Cut out the "Term" and "Definition" flaps.
5. Stack the "Term" flap on top of the "Definition" flap and place on top of the "How..." flap. Secure with glue or a stapler.

Term	**Term**
Term	**Term**
DEFINITION	**DEFINITION**
DEFINITION	**DEFINITION**

Copyright material from Ashley Johnson, *Unlocking the Career and Technical Education Classroom*, 2025, Routledge

Name _____ Date _____ Period_____

_____ _____ _____ _____ _____ _____ _____ _____ **How will understanding this term benefit you?**	_____ _____ _____ _____ _____ _____ _____ _____ **How will understanding this term benefit you?**
_____ _____ _____ _____ _____ _____ _____ _____ **How will understanding this term benefit you?**	_____ _____ _____ _____ _____ _____ _____ _____ **How will understanding this term benefit you?**

Copyright material from Ashley Johnson, *Unlocking the Career and Technical Education Classroom*, 2025, Routledge

Term Table Jams

Using at least five terms from the "Word Wall" write a poem or song. Make sure the terms are used correctly in context with what we are studying. Write your poem/song on the lines around the record on your "Term Table."

List terms from the "Word Wall" included in your poem/song.

Word Wall Matching Game
Front-of-Cards

For each "Word Wall" word, make two cards; one with the written term and one with a drawing to match the term. When finished, shuffle the cards and lay them all face down. Take turns flipping over two cards. When you make a match (term with drawing representing the term) keep the match. The person with the most matches at the end of the game is the winner!

Copyright material from Ashley Johnson, *Unlocking the Career and Technical Education Classroom*, 2025, Routledge

Word Wall Matching Game
Back-of-Cards

Print this page front-to-back with the front-of-card page.

Word Wall Final Assessment Options

For the final assessment of a Word Wall unit, pick one of the following assignment options. No matter what option you choose, make sure you meet the learning objective.

LEARNING OBJECTIVE: Present key concepts in a way that could be used to quickly inform or teach someone else on the topic of the unit.

Word Wall Whisper:
You will create a compelling and engaging, informational presentation for the Word Wall unit. Make sure your presentation includes key concepts to effectively inform your audience on the subject matter of the unit.

Your Word Wall Whisper should include:
- Between two and three minutes of content
- A slideshow to enhance your presentation
- Advice or Action steps learned from the unit members of the audience can use to better their lives
- An introduction, main points, and conclusion
- ALL Word Wall Words

Create a Podcast Episode:
You will create your own podcast episode on the topic of this unit. Make sure your podcast includes key concepts to effectively inform your audience on the subject matter of the unit.

Podcast episode should answer the following questions:
- What were the overall concepts of the unit?
- What information stood out? Why?
- What advice would you give based of the information from this unit?

Podcast episode should include:
- Between two and Three minutes of content
- An intro with music
- An outro with music
- One fake sponsorship mentioned in the episode
- ALL Word Wall Words

Write a Blog Post:
You will write a blog post on the topic of this unit. Make sure your blog post includes key concepts to effectively inform your audience on the subject matter of the unit.

Blog Post should answer the following questions:
- What were the overall concepts of the unit?
- What information stood out? Why?
- What advice would you give based of the information from this unit?

Blog Post should include:
- At least 500 words
- Photos or Graphics that support the information presented (at least two)
- ALL Word Wall Words

Word Wall Final Assessment Rubric

	Novice	Limited	Developing	Mastery
LEARNING OBJECTIVE: Present key concepts in a way that could be used to quickly inform or teach someone else on the topic of the unit.	Student communicates little to no knowledge of key concepts of the unit. No examples of advice or action steps that relate the the unit are given for the reader or audience.	Student communicates limited knowledge of some key concepts of the unit. Limited examples of advice or action steps that relate the the unit are given for the reader or audience.	Student communicates knowledge of the key concepts of the unit. Broad examples of advice or action steps that relate the the unit are given for the reader or audience.	Student communicates mastery of the key concepts of the unit. Specific examples of advice or action steps that relate the the unit are given for the reader or audience.
WORD WALL WORDS: ALL words used in the context of the unit.	Less than 50% of Word Wall words are used in the correct context of the unit.	At least 50% of Word Wall words are used in the correct context of the unit.	At least 75% of Word Wall words are used in the correct context of the unit.	ALL Word Wall words are used in the correct context of the unit.
PRESENTATION: Is the information presented in a professional, engaging and informative way?	The project is very unprofessionally presented, does not inform and is not engaging to the reader or audience. Many distracting errors or mistakes are present.	The project not professionally presented, lacks information and is not very engaging to the reader or audience. Several distracting errors or mistakes are present.	The project is mostly professionally presented, informative and engaging to the reader or audience. Very few and small distracting errors or mistakes are present.	The project is professionally presented, informative and engaging to the reader or audience. No distracting errors or mistakes are present.
REQUIREMENTS: Does the final product meet the guidelines?	Project guidelines are far from being met, including length and supplemental materials (images, audio, slides).	Project guidelines are halfway met, including length and supplemental materials (images, audio, slides).	Project guidelines are close but not fully met, including length and supplemental materials (images, audio, slides).	All project guidelines are met or exceeded, including length and supplemental materials (images, audio, slides).

Copyright material from Ashley Johnson, *Unlocking the Career and Technical Education Classroom*, 2025, Routledge

Book Study Bookmarks

TEACHERS: Before you begin your book study, plan out your reading and chapter due dates. Fill out the bookmark template below and make copies. Give each student a bookmark to help keep them on track with the study.

This bookmark belongs to:	This bookmark belongs to:	This bookmark belongs to:
_____	_____	_____
We are reading:	We are reading:	We are reading:
_____	_____	_____
Chapter — **Due Date**	**Chapter** — **Due Date**	**Chapter** — **Due Date**

Copyright material from Ashley Johnson, *Unlocking the Career and Technical Education Classroom*, 2025, Routledge

Back of Bookmarks

TEACHERS: Print bookmark pages front to back for a double sided bookmark.

QUOTES:	QUOTES:	QUOTES:
THINGS TO REMEMBER:	THINGS TO REMEMBER:	THINGS TO REMEMBER:

Name _____ Date _____ Period ____

Book Study Goals

Before you begin your book study, evaluate what you already know and what you want to know on the subject matter of the book. Then establish goals for the study.

Name of Book:

Subject Matter of Book:

What do you already know about the subject matter of this book?

What do you want to know about the subject matter of this book?

Goal ONE: Create a goal to accomplish by the time you finish this book.

Goal TWO: Create a long term goal you hope to accomplish from the knowledge you gain from this book.

Copyright material from Ashley Johnson, *Unlocking the Career and Technical Education Classroom*, 2025, Routledge

Name _____ Date _____ Period _____

Book Study Chapter Worksheet

For the current chapter of our book study, summarize what you read, define key terms, and quote something that stuck with you.

Name of Book:	Chapter:

List and define at least five key terms from the chapter.	Summarize the chapter by drawing a picture OR writing three sentences.
	Quote something from the chapter that stuck with you. Include the page number.

Copyright material from Ashley Johnson, *Unlocking the Career and Technical Education Classroom*, 2025, Routledge

Name _____ Date _____ Period ____

Book Study Wrap Up

After you finish the book, complete the following questions as we wrap up the book study.

Name of Book:

What did you learn from reading this book?	Summarize the overall theme of the book by drawing a picture or writing five sentences.
Did you accomplish your first goal? Why or why not?	
What steps do you need to implement to achieve your second goal?	**Would you recommend this book to a friend? Why or why not?**

Copyright material from Ashley Johnson, *Unlocking the Career and Technical Education Classroom*, 2025, Routledge

Book Study Final Assessment Options

For the final assessment of our book study, pick one of the following assignment options. No matter what option you choose, make sure you meet the learning objective.

LEARNING OBJECTIVE: Convey the theme and guiding principles of the book and how they are relevant to your current or future life.

Create a Book Jacket:
You will create your own version of the book jacket for this book. You will need to design the cover, spine, and back cover. You can use the *template provided* or use a digital program to create your design (eg. canva.com).

Front cover should include:
- The title of the book
- The author's name
- A one sentence blurb that gives the overall theme of the book
- A picture that works with the theme of the book

Back cover should include:
- A blurb of 5 to 7 sentences (Short summary of what the reader should expect when reading this book)
- A testimonial of 2 to 3 sentences from you (why you liked the book and why people should read it)
- Pictures or graphics that fit with the theme of the book

Book spine should include:
- The title of the book
- The author's name
- A small graphic that fits with the theme of the book

Create a Podcast Episode:
You will create your own podcast episode on the topic of this book. You will need to create a 3 to 5 minute podcast episode discussing the theme and guiding principles of this book.

Podcast episode should answer the following questions:
- What was the overall theme and principles discussed in this book?
- What information stood out? Why?
- Would you recommend this book to a friend? Why?

Podcast episode should include:
- An intro with music
- An outro with music
- One fake sponsorship mentioned in the episode

Write a Book Report:
You will write a book report discussing the theme and guiding principles of the book.

Book report should include:
- An introduction
- Discussion of at least three standout principles and how they are relevant to your life
- A conclusion
- At least 500 words

Book Jacket Template

Back

Spine

Front

Copyright material from Ashley Johnson, *Unlocking the Career and Technical Education Classroom*, 2025, Routledge

Final Assessment Rubrics

	Novice	Developing	Proficient	Advanced
LEARNING OBJECTIVE: Convey the theme and guiding principles of the book and how they are relevant to your current or future life.	Student has **NOT met** the learning objective. Student communicates **little to no mastery** of the guiding principles and theme of the book. No examples are given.	Student is **approaching** the learning objective. Student communicates **partial mastery** of the guiding principles and theme of the book. Examples are given but not specific to the student's own life.	Student has **met** the learning objective. Student communicates **mastery** of the guiding principles and theme of the book and illustrates specific examples of real life application for their own life.	Student has **exceeded** the learning objective. Student communicates **mastery** of the guiding principles and theme of the book and illustrates in-depth, specific examples of real life application and relevance to their own life.
Expectations: Required elements of assignment have been met.	Student has **NOT met** the required elements of the assignment. **Book Jacket:** Cover is missing one or more of the following: title, author, one sentence blurb, and pictures. Back cover is missing one or more of the following: 5-7 sentence blurb, 2-3 sentence testimonial, and pictures/ graphics. Spine is missing one or more of the following: title and graphic. **Podcast:** Length is less than 2 minutes. Two or more questions are not answered. Intro or outro are missing. Fake sponsor is not mentioned. **Book Report:** Length is less than 200 words. No or one standout principle is included. Intro or conclusion are missing.	Student has **partially met** the required elements of the assignment. **Book Jacket:** Cover is missing one of the following: title, author, one sentence blurb, and pictures. Back cover is missing one of the following: 5-7 sentence blurb, 2-3 sentence testimonial, and pictures/ graphics. Spine is missing one of the following: title and graphic. **Podcast:** Length is close to the 3 to 5 minutes parameter. All Questions are answered but not fully explained. Intro and outro are included without but without music. Fake sponsor is not mentioned. **Book Report:** Length close to 500 words. Two standout principles are included. Intro and conclusion are included.	Student has **met** the required elements of the assignment. **Book Jacket:** Cover includes title, author, one sentence blurb, and pictures that display the theme of the book. Back cover includes 5-7 sentence blurb, 2-3 sentence testimonial, and pictures/graphics that fit the theme of the book. Spine includes title and graphic that fits the theme of the book. **Podcast:** Length is between 3 and 5 minutes. All Questions are answered and explained. Intro and Outro with music are included. Fake sponsor is mentioned. **Book Report:** Length is at least 500 words. Three standout principles are included. Intro and conclusion are included.	Student has **exceeded** the required elements of the assignment. **Book Jacket:** Cover includes title, author, one sentence blurb, and pictures that display the theme of the book. Back cover includes 5-7 sentence blurb, 2-3 sentence testimonial, and pictures/graphics that fit the theme of the book. Spine includes title and graphic that fits the theme of the book. It is evident extra time and care was given to produce a thoughtful and attractive product. **Podcast:** Length is between 3 and 5 minutes. All Questions are answered and explained. Intro and Outro with music are included. Fake sponsor is mentioned. It is evident extra time and care was given to produce a thoughtful and professional quality product. **Book Report:** Length is well over 500 words. More than three standout principles are included. Intro and conclusion are included. It is evident extra time and thought was put into the report.

Badges & Brags

_____

Badges:

Brags:

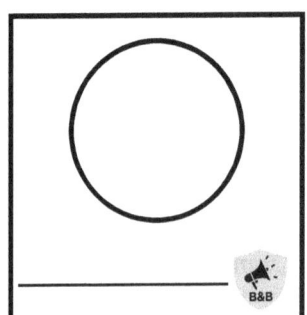

Article Annotations

Name _____ Period ____ Date_____

Article Annotation Worksheet

Use the following annotation markings on your article. Then answer the questions below.

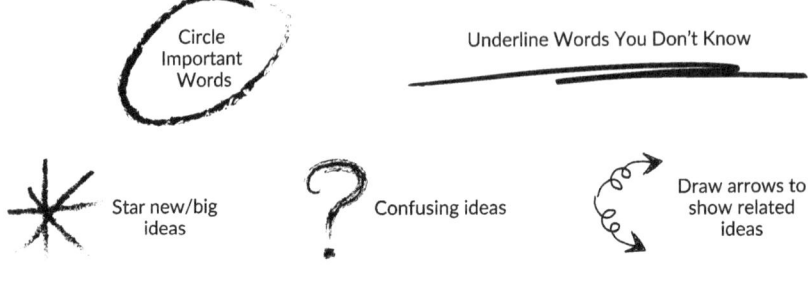

Name of Article _____

What was your big takeaway from this article? Why is it relevant? How will you apply it in your life?

_____
_____
_____
_____
_____
_____

What questions do you have or what questions did the article bring up?

_____
_____
_____
_____
_____
_____

Name: _____ Period _____ Date _____

Article Annotation Rubric

Article Title: _____

	Novice	Limited	Developing	Mastery
Annotations	Article had less than 3 annotation markings.	Article had 3-5 annotation markings.	Article had 5-7 annotation markings.	Article had over 7 annotation markings.
Application to Life	At least 1 question is answered. No application to life is present.	Both Questions are answered but only surface level application is given.	Both Questions are answered and include a reference to life.	Both Questions are answered and include a specific application to life.
Depth of Though	Depth of thought is minimal and not communicated in a clear manner.	Depth of thought is minimal but communicated.	Depth of thought is adequately communicated.	Depth of thought is advanced and carefully planned and communicated.
Further Questions	Little to no effort is given on further questions on the topic of the article.	Further questions about the topic of the article are given.	Proficient thought is present to further questions about the topic of the article.	Higher level thinking is applied to further questions about the topic of the article.

Copyright material from Ashley Johnson, *Unlocking the Career and Technical Education Classroom*, 2025, Routledge

Guest Speakers

Name _____ Period ____ Date_____

Guest Speaker Worksheet

SPEAKER PRE-WORK
Complete BEFORE the guest speaker attend class.
Speaker Name _____
Speaker Occupation _____
List three questions for the speaker.
_____
_____
_____

SPEAKER DAY
Complete while the guest speaker visits.

Key Takeaways	Memorable Quotes

Next Steps	

Copyright material from Ashley Johnson, *Unlocking the Career and Technical Education Classroom*, 2025, Routledge

7

Conclusion

I hope you have found some great resources and lessons to include in your classrooms. These lessons cover a range of topics that can be incorporated into a variety of Career and Technical Education (CTE) classes and can easily be modified to fit into almost any CTE classroom.

The great thing about most of these lessons is you can use them multiple times but in a different way each time. Many are a skeleton that can fit around whatever lesson or unit you are currently working on.

You can use the "Book Studies" lessons for several different books and it won't get stale because each book is different and unique. Same with the "Article Annotations" lesson. Students can use the chapter worksheets to pull out what stuck with them most. And, with multiple final assessments, students have a variety of options to express their important takeaways.

The Quick Pitch Challenge can be used several times a year as a creativity boost or brain cleanse because you will draw different objects each time, making the prototyping completely different. This activity is great to use for team building or right before a break when students are a bit antsy.

The "Word Wall" lesson and assignments can be used in multiple chapters or units, but the words will be different, so it is different each time. The different activities can help students remember important vocabulary words.

Things like the "Business Fair," "Stock Madness," "Children's Book Project," "Professionalism Day," and "Digital Career Portfolio" can be used from year to year because they are different each year and with each student. Creativity can really bloom with these activities.

Gamify your next unit by using the "Badges and Brags." Creating required badges and extra badges can help occupy those students who always finish early. Challenge them to collect as many badges as possible.

Personally, I love using lessons in my classroom that use a rubric and not an answer key. Give your students the freedom to express their knowledge in their own way. Not only will you empower students to take over their own learning, but also you will significantly cut down on the age-old game of students copying each other's work. Nothing is more frustrating to me than putting time and effort into a lesson, only to get the effort of a few while the others just latch on to others' answers. Take that option away. When completing an assignment must be tailored to each student's experiences and opinions, you force students to take responsibility for their own work.

Feel free to use the lessons as is or tweak them to fit your unique classroom needs. Either way, I hope I have been able to save you some time when it comes to preparation.

For Product Safety Concerns and Information please contact our EU
representative GPSR@taylorandfrancis.com
Taylor & Francis Verlag GmbH, Kaufingerstraße 24, 80331 München, Germany

www.ingramcontent.com/pod-product-compliance
Lightning Source LLC
Chambersburg PA
CBHW062128300426
44115CB00012BA/1846